Prepare a Road!

Cowley Publications is a ministry of the Society of Saint John the Evangelist, a religious community of men in the Episcopal Church. Emerging from the Society's tradition of prayer, theological reflection, and diversity of mission, the press is centered in the rich heritage of the Anglican Communion.

Cowley Publications seeks to provide books, audio cassettes, CDs, and other resources for the ongoing theological exploration and spiritual development of the Episcopal Church and others in the body of Christ. To this end, it is dedicated to developing a new generation of theological writers, encouraging them to produce timely, creative, and stimulating publications of excellence, and making these publications available widely, reaching both clergy and lay persons.

Prepare a Road!

Preaching Vocation
Community Voice
Marketplace Vision

Kim L. Beckmann

COWLEY PUBLICATIONS
Cambridge, Massachusetts

Published in the United Sates of America by Cowley Publications, a division of the Society of Saint John the Evangelist. No portion of this book may be reproduced, stored in or introduced into a retrieval system, or transmitted, in any form or by any means—including photocopying—without the prior written permission of Cowley Publications, except in the case of brief quotations embedded in critical articles and reviews.

Library of Congress Cataloging-in-Publication Data:
Beckmann, Kim L., 1957–
    Prepare a road! : preaching vocation, community voice, marketplace vision / Kim L. Beckmann.
        p. cm.
    Includes bibliographical references.
        ISBN 1-56101-206-8 (pbk. : alk. paper)
        1. Preaching.   2. Bible—Homiletical use.   I. Title.
BV4211.3 .B43 2002
251—dc21   2002013453

Scripture quotations are taken from *The New Revised Standard Version* of the Bible, © 1989, by the Division of Christian Education of the National Council of the Churches of Christ in the United States of America. Used by permission.

Cover design: Gary Ragaglia

This book was printed in the United States of America on acid-free paper.

Cowley Publications
907 Massachusetts Avenue
Cambridge, Massachusetts 02139
800-225-1534 • www.cowley.org

Dedication

*To the people of God at Bethany and Trinity Lutheran Churches
and to our communities in Amasa and Stambaugh, Michigan
and with love to my co-pastor and spouse,
Fredric D. Kinsey*

❧ Contents ❧

✒ Acknowledgments ✒

One of the best parts of collaborative preaching is the opportunity to have many partners in my work. I give thanks for my mentors and friends at the Lutheran School of Theology at Chicago and the ACTS Doctor of Ministry in Preaching Program. They opened so many doors to life, faith, and ministry and called this book into being. In particular:

- ✒ Dow Edgerton, who asked, "What book do you want to write?"

- ✒ Dick Jensen, who graciously invited, "Write it!"

- ✒ Jim Nieman, who suggested, "Let this be its voice."

- ✒ And especially David J. Schlafer, who declared, "This is it!" with such absolute conviction that it became so. Thank you, David, for being such a sponsor, pastor, friend, and enthusiastic reader. Without your encouragement, I would not be enjoying this moment.

My preaching colleagues in the program would think themselves unlikely midwives, but I offer thanks to them for pulling this idea out of me one summer day: the steadfast Steve Schwier; Tom Rogers and Carroll Marohl; and Chip Gunsten for leaning into the fishbowl and whispering: "Tell them about the bulldozer!"

Conversations with Paula Knutson and Philip Hefner brought spark and life to this project, a "something more" in their gifts for critical reflection. I am so grateful for the insight of others who read the manuscript for me at various stages of development: Christa Von Zychlin, Ken and Mary Strecker, Brian Baker, Mary Weinkauf, and "Mother Margaret" Johnson, whose check-ins meant the world. I am graced by long-time friends Jay Rochelle, David Rhoads, Sally

Simmel, and Ken Sawyer, who were generous in sharing their expertise at all the right moments. Thanks also to Alison Carrick at Washington University Library for her assistance.

To Kevin R. Hackett SSJE and the staff at Cowley Publications, I give thanks for this opportunity and for their skillful and prayerful publishing. Thanks particularly to my editor, Susan M.S. Brown, for her vast contribution, along with the gift of kindness and the art of cutwork embroidery she brought to this work, which in the end is not mine but ours.

I'm grateful to Larry Schiavo and all who have so freely allowed me to share their stories in these pages. And I am most and for ever grateful to Fred Kinsey, my husband and partner in ministry, who made sure there was orange juice every morning and then shouldered much of my share of the load so that I could reach out and grow. I am rich in friends who offer encouragement and hospitality and thank all of them, especially the Klonowski-Burnet household. For Mom and Dad, sister and brothers, uncles, aunts and extended family, and all who have nurtured me in the sacramental life, thanks be to God.

Many thanks to those largely unknown to me except through their work with which this book is in dialogue. And finally, to those cheering me on from the cloud of witnesses, I feel your benediction.

—Kim L. Beckmann
June 24, 2002
Feast of the Nativity Saint John the Baptist

Not long ago, a friend sent me an email that contained a story about a mother who once found her little boy standing on the open pages of his favorite storybook. Curious, she asked him what he was doing. As he stamped on the pages, unable to give voice to his longings, the mother began to see that he was doing his best to get himself into the story, to be in the book. He wanted to enter its pages and live in its world.

I'm not sure what the mother in this Internet story did to help her son find his own way to become part of the story he loved, to crash through the boundary and extend the limits that words on pages posed for this boy, who was struggling to live within his favorite book, but as a preacher, I would like to know.

Here is another story. This one captured my own childhood imagination:

Martin Luther, fearing for his life, is hidden away in a castle by his friends. Still burning with desire to continue his reforming work, he decides to translate the Bible from "church language," and into the language of the people. Day after day, Luther sits in his cold, grey cell, quill in hand (ink pot always ready for casting at the devil), imagining what would happen if his people could have the Word of God in their own tongue, ready at their lips.

He comes across a word such as "bread." Of course he knows the German word, but he wonders what word the people use for bread—bread they put on their tables every day. He looks out over his desk toward the little stone window and beyond toward the living color of the market square.

Luther disguises himself in a thick cloak and hat and slips out of the quiet castle into the hustle and bustle of the marketplace where the merchants have set up their wares. The housekeepers and the towns-people are out and about, catching up on the latest news. The dogs are running around, and the children are begging for sweets. He hears people haggling over prices, sees lovers strolling arm-in-arm, and observes neighbors fighting about the garbage that has been tossed out the windows. He hangs out by the baker's wagon to listen for the word people use when they're getting their daily bread—just the plain old, everyday, common stuff for their table. His ear suddenly catches a beggar's voice, crying out for a crust.

Later, Luther sneaks back to the castle, passing through the shadows of the alleys and the smells of dinner cooking. He goes back to his little cell and opens his translation to the place in the story where Jesus talked about bread. Luther scribbles in the word he heard, so the people will know that the Bread of Life is bread for them. Common. Necessary. Holy and ordinary. And, above all, for them.

I have not been able to find a written version of this story anywhere. Nor has anyone I've asked heard it. In my search, I've discovered instead that when Luther was translating the Old Testament, he hosted dinner parties to which he invited all the best biblical schol-ars and linguists. And rather than having the village marketplace shape the language of his translation, Luther's Bible was itself the source of the language the German people were to have in common. This solid scholarship does not convince me I'm making this up. To me, it's just another kind of true story. Preachers need both.

In my own sermon-writing cell, surrounded by a feast of commen-tary, I find myself casting a wandering (and wondering) eye out the window toward the village square, where this gospel, will finally have to live. What if the sermon could be conceived in the very soil in which it has to take root?

While many of us consider the Bible to be the favorite storybook into which we want to climb, we nevertheless often find its language inac-cessible, its setting unfamiliar, and the apprehension of its real mean-ings for daily life frustrating to pursue. In our frankly market-driven society, where such a difficult story must compete with many other stories—stories that are both easier to access and seemingly easier to inhabit—the gospel story calls forth faithful and inspired interpreters and equally faithful and inspired tellers.

Perhaps we storytellers of the gospel could take our place squarely in this marketplace. Standing on our street corner, marketing our life-giving wares along with the other vendors, what language, imagery, and narrative forms will we use to allow the biblical voice to be heard above, or perhaps just in the midst of, the lively bustle of the public square?

If, however, we consider the parish preacher to be the only interpreter, the only storyteller, we spread ourselves way too thin. If we consider that the point of the sermon is for hearers to "get it," if sermon speech aims only for the pews—not through them, and through the doors so that the world "gets it," too—we aim way too short. What if parish preachers and everyday preachers together could learn a language we could hold in common, a faith language that would serve us in the common spaces of life?

So along with the best linguists and biblical scholars at my sermon-writing table I seated also the merchants and townspeople, and together we pored over the assigned texts for the day. I seated high schoolers next to grandmothers. Loggers next to lab technicians. The not-yet-committed to church life next to those born in a pew. They all came because they were invited to be part of an experiment, one which required us to be committed to the process for just a few months, a specific number of sermons. And they came because it sounded interesting, different. They stayed as they discovered within themselves a thirst for talking with others about things that deeply mattered in their lives and faith. In the process we had become more interested in the Word and world—and each other. We grew curious about the wheat and the chaff, and what scripture has to say about glory and service. And we viewed it all in light of the stories of our veterans. We learned how we live through grief, and we thought hard about why people flock to the gambling casinos.

One colleague began such a group obligating participants for just one month at a time, after which each member invites someone else in the community to take his or her place. I've led study groups that met for an hour each week to talk about the upcoming sermon. It doesn't matter how you gather people around the Word. The Word accommodates the gathering. The preaching groups you'll meet in these pages were drawn first from one point of my parish, then another. A third group was formed of members from both congregations. We met two weeks to ten days before I would preach the sermon. We spent a good two hours dreaming over the images, asking about the biblical setting, and considering the issues of faith in their jobs, homes, and community.

Like Luther, I listened to the words they used for "bread." Then I slipped out of my castle. I asked them to send me, or take me, into the corners of the market square where I might see these stories at work in the world. Sometimes, we used close translations—the county courthouse for sentences and pleadings for the Unforgiving Servant. Sometimes, we used imaginative, contemporary juxtapositions. For example, the casino setting for the Temple controversy story. Sometimes, we found a connection to people in our community who were living the story as part of their daily lives and ordinary work.

I got to spend Friday mornings at the Pine Cone Café, seeing how news is spread around town. I got to visit the parking lots where kids hang out after "lapping town" in their cars for awhile, and I thought about Nicodemus's coming to Jesus in the night. I got to go to high school football and basketball games and out for Fish Fry at the Hotel Bar. I got to have coffee at many kitchen tables and to do some porch-sitting. I say "got to" because that's how I felt about what I was doing. Privileged. This is the kind of visitation I'd always wanted to do—and the kind I never seemed to get around to. There's the office to clean. There's the newsletter to write. The hospitalized to visit. And, of course, there's always a sermon to prepare. But now "going out" was an assignment, a covenant, a discipline. "I'm sorry. Tonight I have to go to Fish Fry, and then to the basketball game!" That's what the Luther of my story must have been feeling: tired of sitting in that lonely castle tower, eager for any excuse to get away from the books, the desk, and the papers—to get out into the noise and humanity.

This book walks through the sermon-writing process that began when John the Baptist's wilderness call to "Get a road ready for the Lord" took me out on Larry's bulldozer. Opening a logging road with Larry, I tried to see what his daily work could tell us of the advent life. In the space of these pages, we will sit around the table with people like Peggy, Lois, Mel, and Rich—members of my preaching groups discovering the Word taking flesh. We'll go out into the marketplace to experience the Word in action. We'll consider the mystery of sermon development and hear the sermon as preached in the Word's body. We'll reflect on the ways sermons are lived as a Word loosed back on the world. In between, we'll encounter some of those sermons.

The preaching process as it unfolds in these pages represents an experiment in finding ways to break through the barriers of print on page. We will find ways to make the world of scripture a story we can walk into, claim as our own, and share with others, using language that gives voice to our longings and feels comfortable on our lips. Through this process we will also come to remember how God already has broken into our human story, our landscapes, and our lives which are newly discovered as arenas for God's gracious activity in and through us and the created world.

I anticipate our time together in this ongoing dialogue in much the same way I envision my role as parish preacher: as an opportunity for us to throw open as many windows as possible, all the while praying that the Holy Spirit will choose to fly through one of them.

Amen! Come, Holy Spirit!

Chapter 1

A Road in the Wilderness:
Surveying the Text

Every classic lives as a classic only if it finds readers willing to be provoked by its claim to attention.
—David Tracy, *The Analogical Imagination*

All old stories . . . will bear telling and telling again in different ways. What is required is to keep alive, to polish, the simple clean forms of the tale which must be there . . . And yet to add something . . . which makes all these things seem new and first seen, without having been appropriated for private or personal ends.
—A.S. Byatt, *Possession*

The leaders in Jerusalem sent priests and Temple helpers to ask John who he was. He told them plainly, "I am not the Messiah." Finally, they said, "Who are you then? . . . John answered in the words of the prophet Isaiah, "I am only someone shouting in the desert, 'Get the road ready for the Lord!'"
—John 1:19-20,22-23 *CEV*

We've got to start with what's before us. For a preacher, it is the text. For the logger preparing a road in the wilderness, it's that parcel of land to be harvested. In the end, these two tasks are not that different.

I came upon this insight when, one day, the logger and the preacher went to work together. For a while, Larry and I rode around on the bulldozer, but then he wanted to take a walk. Cruising, they call it, when they begin the job, it's when you can't see the trees for the forest. There is no real substitute for getting out and walking it. It might be disorienting at first. That's why we have a compass and a sun chart, which checks the compass against the magnetic pull of the iron ore under our feet. Individual trees begin to emerge and show themselves for what they are: birch, cherry, mature trees, rotten wood, seedlings. Pretty soon the landscape feels like home, and the road that was always there, waiting to be opened, starts to reveal its shape.

Others have been here before us, marking trees that are of value, the hoped-for harvest. The blazes they have made with their colorful paint begin to form a pattern and to reveal the road. We check the boundaries, looking for the surveyor's outline of the parcel. Walking through the woods ourselves verifies the symbols we've seen on the map. It becomes clearer, finally, how to chart the path through high ground and swamp.

Larry and I are squinting together, framing the road that even I can see now. I see it through his eyes: the straightest way, through the subtle openings. Back on the bulldozer, we make landings and skidways, parking places for the pickup trucks, spaces for piling the logs. We need to make room for the people, and for the harvest. Soon, the loggers will arrive.

❦

So we begin our work with the text, cruising it. Others have been here before us, and their markings orient us. Their maps may indicate the high and swampy spots, blazes may point out what those earlier travelers found valuable and ripe for harvest, but there is no substitute for our getting out and walking through the text until its landscape becomes material. Squinting, we let the road that is already there reveal itself to us and prepare us for the good news of Jesus' coming among us.

When we meet Jesus there on the road, we find that this text isn't just marks on paper: it is sacred space, dimensional space. It is a world that is recognizable, livable, and full of possibility. It's a story that we really can step into, just as the little boy in this book's introduction attempted to get inside the pages of his favorite storybook, and we can live in its world.

Alla Bozarth writes that when we let the story show itself to us this way, we are "discovering the real presence of the text."[1] That sounds like communion to me.

Can we survey the text alone? I hope we do, sometimes. I hope we can find quiet mornings or evenings to tramp around in our favorite stories. There is no substitute for knowing the landscape of the Bible deep in our very own bones. But this text, as we come to find out, is also a peopled landscape that invites us into its own dialogue, calling us out of ourselves into community.[2] The story itself makes room for us to come in together. It provides the hospitality of landings for our arrival, opening itself up to differing points of view.

The Bible begins in just this way, providing two distinct stories of the creation of the universe. In Genesis 1, we have a cosmopolitan, aesthetic, ordered story featuring God as a thinker and planner. But Genesis 2 uses local color in an earthy account of humans formed out of the very ground, enlivened by a God who seems to be making it up as God goes along.[3] The final editor of Genesis included (and the people preserved) both stories together as reflections of what it means to be human and to be in relationship with one another, with all creation, and with a loving God. Together, they present a reality Patricia Wilson-Kastner writes is "not a one-dimensional phenomenon . . . but a multifaceted story that can be entered into, told, and heard from varying perspectives." This story and its world represent a "multiverse," she continues, borrowing Jamake Highwater's term.[4] So scripture's own internal dialogue, not experienced apart from the ongoing conversations of those who have gone before us blazing and marking the territory, extends an invitation for us to work collaboratively in discovering the road within.

We can cruise with other preaching colleagues within the dimensions of the text. I know I couldn't do without Margaret and Judy, Nancy, Jon and Wally; they are a community of faith for me. They also serve collectively as my Eli, who helped Samuel recognize and attend to God's Word to him (1 Samuel 3), and as my Elizabeth, who named what was happening within Mary, enabling her to break forth into the *Magnificat* (Luke1:39-56).[5] But I've become convinced that we can't preach without also squinting into a viewfinder with Larry and others like him, seeing through his eyes the road on which Jesus will come to meet us. I want Larry and our friends to join me in cruising the text because

- Discovering the real presence of a text is communion, and we don't celebrate communion in isolation.

- The preacher doesn't own this parcel of text, the community holds it in common.

- A story held in common is less likely to be appropriated for an individual's own ends. If, as Lucy Rose suggests, the sermon is a gathering of people around the Word, how better to prepare than to rehearse this by gathering people around the Word?[6]

- Larry and our other friends are the ones who can help preachers see and hear the sermon as-it-will-be-heard in the marketplace where it has to live—and they are preparing for preaching, too.

- Preparing a sermon collaboratively makes for a discipline for all of us.

It's true that preaching collaboratively means I have to make a date with Larry and keep it faithfully. I can't just take this walk about the text whenever the spirit moves me and only me, whenever the cracks in my schedule permit, or even just not get to it if the week's been especially busy. Same for Larry. But probably we're going to have some kind of weekly Bible study anyway. Barbara Brown Taylor writes about the day it occurred to her that people were not looking for information as much as they were looking to experience God through their encounters with the Bible. She invited the participants in her biblical meditation class to shut their eyes and walk in their imaginations through the stories:

We were scared witless by Lazarus stumbling mummy-blind from his tomb. We handled the precious stones that encrusted the walls of Jerusalem; we dangled our feet in the river of life that ran through the middle of it. We dug our hands into baskets of dried fish and bread, eating from them until our belts cut off circulation. Afterward we compared notes on where we had been and what we had seen, finding out most of us had gone on the same trip, although we remembered different things about it.[7]

Taylor discovered that walking through the texts, as if it were a world that could be inhabited, brought the participants new, visceral understandings of themselves, God, and other people. They saw aspects of the story they had never known before—some the preacher had never seen before, either. When Larry and his friends and the preacher gather around the Word, the text takes on flesh. It gets a life.

There are many designs and possibilities for gathering people around the text.[8] In our own congregational adventure, we worked from the lectionary, though for reasons of tradition, insight, or crisis, or the politics of "breaking" that institutional system, one might decide to work with some other text. Because we chose the lectionary, we began with the prayer of the day, placing the texts in the perimeters of our Sunday and season. And then we read them, walked them, and offered our "first takes" or impressions. We raised our questions. We couldn't see the road yet, but we were able to suspend our panic.

We looked for the other boundary markers, both in the text and in biblical and historical scholarship. We brought to the table our different orienting tools: our faith, our knowledge, our experience. We looked for the blazes of those who had gone before us and we added our own colorful splashes and markings. We cruised the high ground, and we slogged through the swamps of our own lives. We asked what we—and our neighbors—needed from the harvest of this parcel of text. We anticipated at every turn the surprise of happening upon the One we hoped to find all along, the One to whom we could tell the events of the day and who would open our minds to these scriptures.

Then we had coffee.

Miraculously if it hadn't been for all our walking, the road as it will come to be begins to materialize. What do we see? What do we hear? What words and narratives are used? What patterns of speech do the blazes make? What was the way into the story?

I noticed that we already knew the Unforgiving Servant. This guy was a "slimebucket," a "user," a "taker." He "shook down his fellow servants for chump change." Not much would need to be explained. He was a marketplace regular already.[9]

My ears perked up whenever we got the giggles or everyone started talking at once. The energy of laughter, creativity, or even intoxication about an absurd idea, means that the road may be materializing. That's how the road through the story of Jesus' controversy over paying taxes to Caesar began to reveal itself. Someone was reminded of the gambling casinos that dot our landscape. Electricity shot through the room. What if we honestly looked at (gasp) gambling? The boldness of even talking about the casino at church excited us. What if Jesus were asked about the sticky issues of the "lawfulness" of Christians' gambling? What if Jesus himself were to walk into the casino? What if the *pastor* were to walk in there? Would she wear a clerical collar or go incognito? Wouldn't it be hilarious if the pastor were to win the jackpot and end up on TV? The excitement around the table tipped me off that a sermon headed in this direction— a sermon-as-it-would-be-heard in a community with issues surrounding the church and gambling—might gain a hearing in the marketplace. This might be a story we would be able to get into.

Each group finds a different way to put flesh on the texts. For this particular group, "the road" started to emerge through the focus on local and contemporary landscape. The members of another group were more likely to see the road when they cruised the spiritual landscape of their own experience and encounters with God and shared with one another what they had observed there.

In this group, during a single week's walk through the texts, we considered the question of faith in the midst of injustice, hardship, and cruelty; the overwhelming nature of public events out of our control; and the challenging aspects of the countercultural life of discipleship (Luke 17:5-10, Habakkuk 1:1-4). The group was quick to focus on the pressing problems that TV has made as vivid as Habakkuk's visions: Kosovo, the Clinton sex scandals, the murder of Matthew Shepard, school violence. Now we could add the Twin Towers of the World Trade Center. Afghanistan. Iraq. Like the prophet, they asked, "Why do we have to look at it?" Mel confessed that sometimes in bed at night, he agonizes, "Is there really a God, with all that is happening? I know there is a God, but where is he?" Members of the group began to share their stories of feeling God's absence, the inability to pray, the sense that they had lost their faith, or that it had been stolen. Slowly, the group turned toward the causes of pain in the world and our lives. Peggy wondered whether God might be like a parent who lets kids discover for themselves, making them take a stand, rather than fixing things for them. "Maybe if enough people do this, what we're doing, something will change." Lois added, "Maybe we have to put ourselves out there, with the courage and the face of Jesus, talking about our faith and not holding back. Maybe *we* are Habakkuk's billboard."

I held my breath when we came to the lessons about our beliefs concerning the resurrection of the dead (Luke 20:27-38) and Job's cry for justice (Job 19:23-27). No one was interested in the backstory of the Sadducees' riddle about the afterlife and why Jesus' answer was such a coup. We just wanted to cry and laugh together about our immediate experiences with grief and loss. We wanted to know what life was like for our departed loved ones, whether we were going to be angels, and if we would have jobs in heaven. Rich, who had lost his mother in a car wreck the previous Christmas Eve, was very quiet until the end, when he said that he wanted some sort of guarantee. Mel looked Rich in the eye and pointed to the last line of the gospel with which we were wrestling: "For he is not a God of the dead, but of the living, for to God, all of them are alive." One by one, the group members testified to the wrenching power of grief, loss, and tragedy and the earth-shattering surprise of resurrection. Lois and Peggy, who had been down that road, were especially effective, helping Rich to see, he said, that "grief is something we *live* through."

This way of walking through the texts called to mind a Native American fleshing stone Lois had once shown me. Jagged teeth had been cut out of the smooth, heavy black stone and a well had been carved to fit the heel of a hand that would apply pressure. This rough tool was used to scrape flesh from the hide of an animal so that the hide, once dried, could clothe or house human bodies. Our gatherings, where we were scraping away the flesh that was on the texts, making of it something new with which to clothe ourselves, reminded me of the work—the applied pressure—behind Lois's fleshing stone. We cried; we scraped away at the story. We wailed our laments; we scraped away at the story. In time, our cries and the cries of the faithful witnesses of scripture became the same lament. It was in our shared tears and the scraping together that the road opened up for us. Taking the fleshing stone to the text, we created a common space there for all our grief, fears, and finally, faith.[10] Hope for the future, the hope that is within us, within the story, clothed us in a new way for our walk in the world.

Put another way, the story is "refleshed" in our gathering around it.[11] Sometimes we looked at the story, and it seemed so dead, so old, so cold, that we wondered whether those bones could ever live. Then one person would breathe a word, maybe just a tentative, little, breathy word about something she might have seen in the story, something she'd wondered about, something that had happened. And the word took on flesh. Sinew. A little muscle. And then maybe, out of nowhere, the story became so alive it was shocking.

It happened that way one day for the group who was delving into the biblical background and trying to live in the story in its own rich textures. We spent some time on the image of the "well" that appears in an Advent text from Isaiah: "With joy you shall draw water from the wells of salvation." We talked about the encounters of John the Baptist with the "brood of vipers" at the river and his winnowing fork and threshing floor. But it was difficult for us, the people who would be hearers and tellers of this sermon today, to find a way into this story.

Just when we were nearly certain there was no road in this parcel of wilderness, Stacy, a ninth grader, responded to my last-ditch question about what good news might be here for the community:

*You don't have to give up everything, just your extra to some-
one who doesn't have the basics. Just be fair. You're not being
asked for too much. Also, the well is the place of the personal
and the profound. It's about things like losing your faith, or
facing an unwanted pregnancy. You could combine the well
with the gospel. It's like being at the river, and the tax collec-
tors had expectations—they were looking into the well, fear-
ful as outcasts to go to the holy place. Also, it was scary,
wondering, am I chaff, or am I wheat? Look down into the
unknown of the well. This river is a place we all meet. We are
maybe all in our own little groups, a little angry, but we all
face the font together.*

Stacy's sermon to her community still takes my breath away. When
we squint into the viewfinder with Larry and his friends like Stacy,
we may even get our sermon written for us. But that point of view
would not take seriously enough Larry's and Stacy's work and responsibility to be preparing their own sermons for life in the world. Dietrich Ritschl claims that members of the community have a
responsibility for proclaiming the gospel during the week and that
their proclamation is not distinct from the preacher's.[12] Why not prepare for our sermons together? Just as gathering a microcosm of the
marketplace around the Word offers the Sunday morning preacher
an opportunity to preview the sermon-as-it-will-be-heard in the pews
and beyond, these gatherings offer those who preach with their words
and with their lives on Monday morning an opportunity to rehearse
engaging one another in the language of faith.

Perhaps it is the lively dimension in the multiverse of scripture itself
that opens things up for us as we start crowding around the
viewfinder. Or perhaps it is just the crowding. Either way, it seems
that when we start cruising the texts together, we begin to realize that
there is lively space between us, too, in our own perspectives and
voices. We notice one another more and more.

Some people call that point of encounter the interface.[13] What if it
is our own skin, the thin boundary between self and others, that forms
the interface between the gospel text and the world? What if this is
how the text gets a life?

For the first time within the space of their married life, within the space of their own home, Gary and Ruth found themselves talking about God. Marriage and home newly became for them that sacred space where the story lived. Sheila found herself talking about her faith with people in the church to whom previously she'd said only, "Good morning." All the group members were surprised to find they could share their hopes and fears, their dreams and griefs, and find them echoed in one another's stories and in the biblical stories that had evoked them.

The preaching groups also began to realize that the Word was seen and heard differently by younger and older members, men and women, lifelong members and new members, people inside and outside the church, people from a range of ethnic, socioeconomic, and educational backgrounds and political orientations. We started to look through one another's eyes to see the road on which Jesus comes to us. We learned to speak to one another about what we were seeing, and we learned to listen, to see the world, and to hear the possibilities that the good news offered each one of us.

It wasn't always easy. With a shock of recognition, Sheila found herself bumping up against the interface of story, world, and our own skins:

> I had to overcome some of my personal prejudices when ideas were put forth for marketplace experiences, especially the National Guard. How could I forget that members of this organization are everyday people who have something to teach me? Haven't I learned by now that I have something to learn from almost everyone I meet?

We learned that the concepts we had constructed of *us* and *them—the* military, scientists, youth today, vs. the world of the gospel—simply didn't hold up. Lab technicians, high schoolers, and National Guard members had gathered at the same table and were struggling with the same Word to take with them into the world. As Stacy would said, we face the font together.

In this way, we began to prepare the road we saw emerging, the road on which Jesus might come into our lives and into our world today.

We started asking ourselves where that Word was alive in our community now, looking even in places and to people we wouldn't have thought had anything in common with this story. Then the members of my group assigned me "field trips" to places where I could look and listen for the story.

They told me that their hardest job was to come up with the field trips. "What do you mean, 'marketplace'?" they asked. At first, I really didn't know. I could only tell them the Luther story that had started me on this quest.

"That's what I mean when I say marketplace,"[14] I told them. "Like the old village square. Or the old town commons. The places where we gather to do business, go for brunch, argue or protest for justice, attend communal happenings, or enjoy the sun on a spring day. Send me to the people in our community who can help us see that the 'bread' of this story is for us. Send me to people who can help us find ways to share the news of Jesus' real presence in this story and in our lives."

I'm lucky. In one of the small towns of my two-point parish, the places that we can consider common space, or common ground, are still fairly cohesive. We have "the store," "the café," "the movie," "the gas station," "the post office." We have several bars. And exactly the same number of churches. In the other town, our gathering spaces are more spread out. But I remember from when I lived in New York City, people who live in Manhattan divided themselves up into little neighborhoods that have "the grocer," "the park," "the subway station," "the bakery," and "the deli" where more often than not, they run into their neighbors. Though these gathering grounds may be disappearing as we multiplex or cocoon, and though the gathering grounds are being reconfigured and reinvented in areas like cyberspace or malls, it is worth discovering and lifting up these spaces.

Later, we realized that what I was calling "marketplace" might better be called "commonspace." Certain kitchen tables in town were clearly common space. Everyone could place themselves at that table. Such commonspace makes all our kitchen tables common gathering space.[15] We discovered that people and their lives could also be commonspace—related to a memory, event, or the embodiment of a particular quality the community holds in common. Certainly TV is a marketplace, and shared or commonspace, as we tune to episodes or events that become cultural meeting grounds. TV also extends our idea of community in widening circles that can encompass the global village.

We discovered these commonspaces, gathering grounds of the marketplace, as we saw the road emerging that let us into the gospel story to make places for people and the harvest. It was exciting when we began to see where we were going.

But it's also true that the scariest moment comes at the end of this chance to cruise the text with the preaching group. Because when the meeting ends with my saying, "Go in peace, serve the Lord," I realize that this time, I have to go out there too. The Luther in my story, after all, was taking a risk by going outside. He had reason to fear for his life beyond the walls of the castle. It's scary for me because I realize in a new way what it's like for those who hear my sermons, who go out those doors on Sunday morning. I realize that for them the walls of the church building are no longer the boundary between gospel and the world. Stained glass and steeple are not the only icons of the faith; God's light shines through their lives with equal beauty and clarity. And now, we, I am going out there, too. James Nieman expresses both the terror and the necessity of this going out:

> . . . our hearers simply will not go where our message leads if we aren't willing to go there ourselves. What can it mean to our parishioners when we claim the centrifugal direction of the gospel, only to remain behind at the doors of the church waving, "Have a nice trip! Be careful out there!" I guarantee you, they will grasp that message and draw the appropriate conclusions. "Faith in the world is impossible," they will think, "Abandon hope, all ye who venture forth."[16]

I've encountered something similar when we've had outdoor worship services. In church, the music and our voices reverberate and embolden us, making us feel one and mighty. Outside, it all sounds feeble. Maybe a little out of place. We feel exposed. A little silly. But once, during an outdoor worship service this summer, I noticed a little boy peering over the fence at us from his backyard. He had climbed up there, curious to see what we were doing outside. He watched us for quite a while.

∾∾

Months had passed since that summer worship. A week had gone by since my group had cruised the text and sent me out. Now it was December, and I was staring through the church window at the motionless bulldozers next door. They were supposed to tear down Saint Mary's Church as soon as hunting season was over. Watching the demolition was supposed to be my field trip for an Advent sermon on ruined cities and God's restoration. But it was already Wednesday, and there was no sign that these dozers were doing anything soon. So much for that sermon! Staring out the window, I sifted through the lessons. "Prepare a road in the wilderness."

I picked up the phone. "Bruce! Anybody you know making new logging roads?" "Well," he said, "you could call Larry. I heard him on the radio today calling for a bulldozer up Smokey Lake way, so I suspect something's happenin' up there. But don't forget, it's Wednesday, sauna night."

I caught Larry just as he was coming through the door after his steam, and I asked what he was up to the next day. He was planning on opening up a road.

So I am going, too. I am going out. I'll be bulldozing with Larry.

NOTES

1. Bozarth, *The Word's Body*, 33.

2. *Ibid.*, 13. Bozarth makes Walter Ong's point that all speech is an invitation to dialogue, "to enter into its ambiance and meet it from within" rather than remaining an outside observer.

3. McCurley, *Proclamation Commentaries*, 10–16. This characterization, and McCurley's suggestions of the appeal of this second creation story with its locality, "earthiness," and "marketplace" languages, in many ways helped launch this preaching experiment.

4. Wilson-Kastner, *Imagery for Preaching*, 35. Jamake Highwater's concept of "multiverse" (as opposed to the mathematical logic of the "universe") is cited here to describe the ways in which realities can assume different relationships and forms, depending upon the perspectives from which they are viewed.

5. Schlafer, "Serving as an 'Eli' or an 'Elizabeth': Listening Preaching Colleagues into Graceful Sermon Speech."

6. Rose, *Sharing the Word*, 93.

7. Taylor, *The Preaching Life*, 47.

8. McClure, *The Roundtable Pulpit*, 67–72, and Gunsten and Schwier, *Partners in Preaching*.

9. Hermeneutics are necessary only when there is something about the language of the text that keeps the word-event of the text from happening for us, says Gerhard Ebeling, as explained in Jensen, *Telling the Story*, 64. Gathering a microcosm of the marketplace around the text gives preachers a rare opportunity to sift out those places where lines between text and life need to be drawn by the preacher from those places in the text where explanation merely complicates or deadens.

10. Tracy, *Blessed Rage for Order*, 78. This kind of common space is probably what Hans-Georg Gadamer once defined as the "fusion of horizons" in the final moments of a text's interpretation. Tracy summarizes this phenomenon as the ability to overcome the "strangeness" of another horizon, not through putting yourself in the author's cultural situation, but by experiencing in the here-and-now the author's basic human vision and experience of being-in-the-world.

11. Rose, *Sharing the Word*, 72. Rose cites John Halvorson's term here for the sermon as the "refleshing" of the text.

12. Ritschl, *A Theology of Proclamation*, 126. Ritschl's work in this regard is also featured in Rose, *Sharing the Word*, 93–94, 96, 98.

13. Alla Bozarth discusses interface in *The Word's Body*, 113–4.

14. Miller, *Marketplace Preaching: Returning the Sermon to Where it Belongs*. For Miller, marketplace means the unchurched world, those outside the church walls.

15. Chopp, *The Power to Speak*, 109. If kitchen tables can also be included in this understanding of the marketplace as our common-spaces of interaction, then Chopp's concern that the spheres of men and women are divided into public space and the private realm can be brought into a different economy of interaction as spaces where God is present, where God acts.

16. Nieman, "Preaching That Drives People Out of Church," 114.

Sermon

Is It Lawful for a Christian To Gamble?

The Pharisees ask Jesus "Is it right to pay taxes to Caesar, or not?" (Matthew 12:15–22)

Jesus walked into the casino at Watersmeet. But in the entrance, with its majestic pillars and domed ceiling, Jesus found himself reminded of the last day he walked into the Temple at Jerusalem.

It wasn't just the pillars at the casino that reminded him of the Temple. It was also the hustle and bustle of the people. The Temple had never been just a house of worship. It had also been a gathering place, a place where folks met and talked about the issues of their day. Rabbis held forth, and people came to see what was happening, to meet their neighbors, to make the scene.

At Passover, the crowd would become so thick people could hardly move. The Temple security would look sharp, and Roman soldiers would be posted around all the entrances. The uniforms here at the casino looked a little different, but that was about all. Jesus joined the press of the weekend crowd at Watersmeet.

Delicious smells were coming from the casino restaurant. He had heard that the wild rice soup was out of this world, but it was steak he was smelling. The waiters and waitresses were hard at their work of serving, but they seemed to be smiling. He'd seen that look before: in the Temple courtyard where the animals for sacrifice were bought and sold. People earned a living for their families this way, and they were always grateful for lots of customers.

Near the animal stands were the tables where the money changers could be found. They exchanged Roman money—with its idolatrous head of the emperor and the inscription declaring the emperor the son of God—for Temple tokens, the house currency. In the casino now, Jesus walked by the casino cashier, where paper money was being exchanged for chips and coin rolls. He saw a woman put on a pair of latex gloves. "The money here is filthy dirty," she explained to Jesus.

Some things seemed different. The sounds were different here at the casino. Instead of people and animals, vendors and rabbis, there was the sound of metal on metal, coins in and coins out, footfalls and voices hushed by carpet, and the faint music of the spinning reels. Small bursts of laughter or cries of excitement occasionally came from the blackjack tables, where the dealers' hands seemed to float the cards.

The casino columns led not to an altar, but to a display of a brand-new Dodge Dakota pickup and some shiny new snowmobiles. "Good luck! You'd look good in one of those snowmobiles!" someone said to Jesus, as he stopped to look at these offerings raised up under the dome.

It was there that people who knew Jesus spotted him. Some looked stunned to see him. "Jesus, should you be in a gambling casino?" they asked. Some turned away guiltily, hoping Jesus hadn't seen them. Others were happy to see him, happy to see Jesus anytime, anywhere. A group—out from work—stopped by to tell him how they had done that night and to talk about how the last Sunday's Temple talk on stewardship had gone.

Word spread that Jesus was in the casino, and a crowd gathered. "What about it, Jesus?" They put him to the test. "Is it lawful for a Christian to gamble? Is it a sin to come to the casino?"

Jesus had faced this kind of question before. Back in the Temple, it had been the Pharisees and the Herodians trying to catch him in the cross fire. The hot issue was whether someone could be a good Jew and pay taxes to Rome.

The Herodians were Jews who felt their best interests lay in making friends with the ruling Romans. Look, they argued, the very Temple in which they were standing was being refurbished beautifully by Herod. Why not pay taxes? So what if someone paid with coins that had the emperor's head on them? Religion has nothing to do with it, they argued. Their position was that it was a way to get ahead. An easier living could be had. What does it hurt?

Jesus saw that their way of life, the false rosy outlook, and their brush with power had trapped them. Take care, Jesus thought. Don't bet the farm that *this* will save you.

The Pharisees, on the other hand, were pretty popular for suggesting that Jews shouldn't pay the Roman tax on every adult. Who wants to pay taxes, especially to an invading nation, a pagan nation? And, with money that any good Jew would have found filthy to the touch—with that head of Caesar and an inscription proclaiming him a god. Jesus saw the ways that legalism, their tendency to see everything as black or white, good or evil, had entrapped them. Take care, Jesus thought, that your own high standards don't come back to bite you in the butt. Then he asked the Pharisee who stood closest to him to show him the coin. They all had a laugh as the man pulled it out of his back pocket before he could figure out he'd been caught in his own trap.

It was a no-win situation back at the Temple then, and it was shaping up like a trap this time, too. Obviously, there were those among the crowd who wanted to hear a strong word from Jesus against gambling and the casinos. Then, there were those who wanted Jesus to say that there was nothing wrong with it. How to answer without offending someone? "Come on, Jesus, inquiring minds want to know! Yes or no? It couldn't be more simple!"

Jesus thought about what he had seen and heard. The come-ons and the promotions to entice . . . and . . . groups of seniors who had gathered on a bus to enjoy each other's company and get out of the house.

He saw people enjoying the soup, an evening out . . . and . . . high rates of interest charged on borrowed money, money people grow desperate for.

He'd seen the vacant, absorbed faces of people staring into the colorful machines, mesmerized by the chance of hitting it big, frantically playing as many machines at one time as they could . . . and . . . he'd seen husbands and wives kidding each other over the blackjack table, having fun and able to walk away.

He'd seen native peoples abandon their heritage . . . and . . . he'd seen the new schools, better housing, and more reliable transportation that had benefitted the whole tribe.

He'd heard the people who argued that the Native Americans, sovereign nations or not, should pay taxes on the earnings . . . and . . . the same people, who either didn't know they should or just didn't think they should report their winnings to the sovereign IRS.

Jesus saw guards, waitresses, cashiers, and hotel clerks who were happy just to have a job to feed their families . . . and . . . Jesus saw people who had lost it all here—homes, families, health, perspective, life savings—and ruined their lives.

The scene took him back to that day in the Temple. And it occurred to him that some things never change. Jesus looked at those who were so quick to judge others on the basis of what seemed so black and white and so clearly as the moral high ground for themselves. He saw how they could be trapped in their own legalisms. And self-righteousness has such a vicious backlash when it turns out that the world is a messy, human place. The lines can't be drawn as simply as we had hoped. Gloves can't be pulled on to keep us from being involved in the workings of the world.

Then Jesus looked at those who were so quick to embrace the casino scene without reflecting on it: they were so easily trapped by its false and empty promise. Trapped by the attraction of the neon, the snowmobiles, and the jackpot that is always around the corner, always in the next roll of the dice, the spin of the reel or wheel or deal. Lured by the false hope that the casino offers a way out for the hopeless, the lonely, the bored, or the empty—those ripe to be trapped by the greed and ensnared by the gambling. Feeling that all this has nothing to do with faith—it's just play time. Wanting to keep God out of it because to have God involved would make them feel vaguely uncomfortable or ashamed.

No question there is good and evil in this world, thought Jesus. But the difference between them is more subtle than we imagine. The answer is not so simple as just lining faith up on one side and the world on the other and letting them duke it out. We just trap ourselves on one side or another.

There's only one way out of the trap, thought Jesus. We need to draw our lines, our lives, differently. We need to draw not lines of faithfulness and worldliness but lives as a circle. A circle in which our lives come from God and are going toward God. A circle of time over which God is sovereign—Lord of all, Lord always! A circle from which we are called to discern, in any situation, in any realm we find ourselves—in school, work, government, play, even in the casino if we go—how we honor God in all things, live our faith, and practice the stewardship of our whole lives.

The question is not whether casinos are good or bad; the question is, can those who find gambling dark and evil name God Lord and sovereign even of the casinos? Can they give God power and imagination to choose any instrument to work God's will for God's world?

And, can those who gamble at the casinos name God the Lord even of the casinos and the time and money they choose to spend there?

Can we all become more whole by taking a moment to bring God into our lives in every situation? Can we set aside our snap judgments and our vague shame, our sense that faith is here and the world is over there? Can we instead make a decision that names God as the center of our whole lives, sovereign over the whole world? That decision acknowledges that there is no corner of our lives or our world that God does not know, does not rule over.

Can they find wholeness, Jesus wondered, by giving themselves and their world up to a God who can bring even life and death together, who can make weal and create woe, form light and create darkness, who does all these things like no other can?

Finally, Jesus turns to those who are shocked and surprised to find him in the casino—either because they thought he shouldn't be there or because he found *them* in the casino when they never thought they'd have to meet *him* there! And while they hold their breaths, waiting for the answer, he asks them a question instead: "Show me the chip used for gambling in this casino. Whose image is stamped on here, and whose title?"

They answer, "The casino logo is on here, and the name of the casino."

Then he says to them: "Give, therefore, to the casino the things that are the casino's."

And then he asks them another question. The one that has the ultimate importance for all of their lives. "And you," Jesus asks, "Whose image is stamped on you?"

"God's!" they say. "We're stamped out in God's image, the image of the God who created light and darkness, the whole world, all that there is, seen and unseen."

"And whose title do *you* bear?" Jesus asks.

They say, "Christ's! We were named children of God. We are sealed with the Holy Spirit, marked with the cross of Christ forever, to bear his creative and redeeming word through all the world."

And Jesus says, "Then give to God the things that are God's." Amen.

Chapter 2

What Do You See? What Do You Hear?
Relating the Text to the Marketplace

WORK OF GOD

14th chapter of Zechariah: On that day there shall be inscribed on the bells of the horses, "Holy to the Lord." And the cooking pots in the house of the Lord shall be as holy as the bowls in front of the altar; and every cooking pot in Jerusalem and Judah shall be sacred to the Lord of hosts.

Collect: Keep us mindful that everything is holy to you and that all people and things are vessels of your presence.
—Morning Prayer, *The Benedictine Prayer Book*

The primary preaching of the Christian community occurs not in pulpits, but in the sacred space of the encounters of our ordinary daily lives and relationships. It is there that we lose heart, betray one another, give up our integrity, declare war, or withhold amnesty. But it is also there that we speak words of love, foster hope, make commitments, grant forgiveness, take stands, and give witness.
—Mary Catherine Hilkert, *Naming Grace*

When John heard in prison what Christ was doing, he sent his disciples to ask him, "Are you the one who is to come, or should we expect someone else?" Jesus replied, "Go back and report to John what you hear and see: The blind receive sight, the lame walk, those who have leprosy are cured, the deaf hear, the dead are raised, and the good news is preached to the poor."
—Matthew 11:2–5 *NIV*

Larry and the other loggers keep early hours. In the dark, I scrounge around on my closet floor hoping to find something that will pass for logging gear, appropriate bulldozing wear. I try not to think about how early it is and how I will be outdoors all day, exposed to the elements. It is December. It is snowing. This is Larry's life.

It is just barely light, but I've found my way down the forest road where Larry is waiting for me in his pickup truck. The engine is running, and it's actually pretty toasty inside. Larry has brought donuts. Coffee. "Every day a picnic in the wilderness," he tells me.

Larry is kind of excited to have me along. But I can tell he's kind of nervous too. He is proud to have his pastor come to see him at his work. But he is also at a loss as to what he can possibly offer me. He knows that I am here to prepare a sermon for Sunday and that it will have something to do with roads. I tell a little about the season of Advent and preparation. I say a little about John the Baptist and getting the road ready. But he still can't see how my sermon and what he does fit together. It doesn't help that I can't really explain it to him and that I'd be nervous about that if I weren't already feeling a little anxious about bulldozing. I try to release the tension for both of us. "Let's just see what happens," I suggest, and I pull on my gloves as I climb out of the truck.

On the bulldozer, I can't believe the roar, the vibration. Larry gives me a pair of little yellow earplugs, but all they do really is drive the rumbling inside. The whole earth trembles.

The iron teeth of the tractor treads bite into the earth. Larry lifts the plowblade high. The aspen whips bend and break. The small trees fall, offering up their roots and secret places, giving way to make a road into the wilderness. The spruce tree shudders in surprise and shakes off all its snow before it crashes to the earth before us. I am leaning back hard in the seat now. Splinter and crack, the treetops become so much brush in which the squirrels and chipmunks will run and play come spring. The scent of crushed balsam reminds us that Christmas is just around the corner.

I am getting accustomed to the roar and rumble, lulled almost to drowsiness as the dozer rocks and sways over the rough terrain, mesmerized by the sights and sounds of bulldozing with Larry. Suddenly, he switches off the engine; the silence is deafening. Larry breaks that silence with good news: "I almost forgot to tell you!" Roused, I remove the earplugs to hear the announcement. "Karen is having her baby today!" Larry's brother-in-law Jim had called him on the CB radio earlier that morning. Jim was already on his way to attend the birth of this long-awaited first grandchild. The scent of fresh-cut Christmas tree is still in the air. The falling snow seems to be playing "Silent Night." Karen's baby is on the way! I can hardly believe it. The earth trembles, the roar resumes as Larry fires up the dozer with new purpose.

Larry puts the plowblade down and scrapes the earth raw. Unable to see what's right in front of him over the hood of the dozer, he is blind to the immediate future but alert to what lies ahead—hazard trees and snags, widow-makers that break and fly. With his hand on the lever, Larry teases out the rocks more by feel than by sight, his eye on a plow corner lest the blade dip and dig in. We slice into a century-old white-pine stump, logged in the days of horses and sleighs and crosscut saws. Out of this stump, a scraggly but tenacious little balsam is growing.

Alongside me, the soil rises dark brown, like modeling clay formed and reformed, turned over, overturned. Bright ferns and tumbled moss make starling splashes of green in the December landscape, tossed up on the snowy margins, displaced. The road is a scar, a loss, but it is surprisingly rich, anticipatory, and fertile, at the same time. I am stunned to realize that the air smells like springtime, the way my garden smells when I dig it up after its winter slumber. It's the smell of new life.

It is a thrilling but disturbing experience. This, then, is getting the road ready. Although I enjoy my wood furniture, my bookcases, not to mention the books themselves (and this page, for that matter), I do not like breaking open the forest landscape in this noisy, ugly way. Not even for the harvest that will make so much—and even my own paycheck—possible. I think of Karen and what she must be experiencing as she labors toward new life. The shuddering, the furrowing, the sounds and smells and sights of the new life that will change her landscape, too, forever.

Larry is backdragging the plowblade now, and the road becomes smoother and level. Opened to the cold and frost, the newly vulnerable earth will harden and bear the traffic of truck and traveler. Perhaps the deer, weary of this winter's haunch-high snow, will also use this path and nibble on the tender branches now within reach along the roadway. Every day a picnic in the wilderness.

We are done for the day. Larry, anxious still, wants to know whether there is anything else he can do for me. "No," I tell him. "I think I have what I need." I thank him for the day, for showing me what John the Baptist is talking about, for letting me experience God's good news with him. I invite him to come to church on Sunday. Larry is unsure of his plans, but he tells me he'll let me know what he hears about Tom and Karen's baby.

I'm about to get into my car when Larry remembers the camera. He keeps it in the glove compartment of the truck because he never knows what he's going to see out there.

❦❦

What do we see? What do we hear out there with Larry?

The preacher who ventures beyond the church doors first notices just how very real is the world in which the gospel lives. It smells of diesel, dirt, and donuts. The marketplace lives in "real" time—as real as your alarm clock and the time it takes Karen's baby to make its way into the visible world. The world works with concrete and situational, not abstract, materials. I drink a thermos of coffee and realize that there is not even an outhouse in the wilderness with Larry. Really. Aides arrive for work at the nursing home and discover that every resident has the flu. We work with chainsaws, bed sheets, spreadsheets and— most significantly—with people. The marketplace deals, for the most part not with print language but with incarnated language. This *is* the commonspace where we utter our betrayals, grope for integrity, cheer one another on, rise and fall in the face of petty and gross injustices, and order take-out for lunch.

Here, where church walls are opened out and flesh and blood—your flesh and blood—is the point of interface between the gospel and the world, it becomes freshly evident that what I can carry with and within me is the only resource I bring to the lively encounter. Out in the forest with Larry, I cannot run back to the office to check a concordance, grab a lectionary, consult a commentary, or fire up Quick-Verse. Larry does not have a copy of my last week's sermon folded up with the sun chart in his flannel shirt pocket for handy reference against magnetic distortions of reality. We are exposed to the elements out there, Larry and I. Unless I am prepared to go into the world carrying an IDB* in a backpack, I need to realize how light and portable, permeable and permutable the Word is in fleshly interface out there where Larry has to do his preaching.

There is really no substitute for sneaking out of Luther's drafty castle and cruising the text of the marketplace ourselves, for walking through its peopled landscape. I can't just squint into the scriptural viewfinder with Larry and his friends. I have to go out on the dozer with him to see and hear how the dead really are raised by the One who comes to us on the road. Now we see two-dimensional symbols on a map lose their representative nature and become concrete, alive, vivid, real. Going out to bulldoze with Larry breaks open the road on which Jesus is coming to us with the power of new life. The experience opens landings and skidways for us, breaking through the thicket of words on a page into the world of the gospel story we are longing to inhabit.

Just as we discovered that the road was there all along, we discover also that God is already there. Faith is already there. The story, the Word is already there.[1] It's there in the announcement of new life on the way. It's there in the revealed truth that there is no new life without death and disruption. It's there in the scrappy little balsam that grows out of the hundred-year-old pine stump. It's there in Larry's preparing the road, helping us to learn something new about our faith through what we discover together. God is also there, faith is there, simply in the witness of Larry's day-by-day competence as a bulldozer operator in his Work of God in the world.[2] On this day, Larry's coffee cup is as sacred a vessel as the chalice on the altar.

*Interpreter's Dictionary of the Bible

This orientation toward the world, suggests F. Dean Lueking, hinges on a kind of openness to what is there to be discovered in recognizing the gospel story that is already there, by being so well-steeped in it ourselves, the story becomes fully apparent to us in the marketplace encounter.[3] Richard Thulin describes learning how as preachers, we are called to notice our own lives in light of God's judgment and grace. We become ever more aware of God's presence in other peoples' daily lives in such a way that God is revealed as the center of every life.[4] In venturing into the marketplace together, we practice these orientations toward the scriptures, our own lives, and others, rehearsing the story that is deep within our bones and alive within the world and our encounters, increasingly experiencing God as the center of all life.

What are we seeing and what are we hearing when we go to work with Larry? Mary Catherine Hilkert would say that we're seeing the world as graced and the community entrusted with the gospel.[5] She would say that when we go out to listen in the marketplace, we are listening for "an echo of that gospel." We are looking for "fragments of salvation." We are looking for the Spirit of God so that we can "name grace."[6] In the marketplace, as in the scriptural text, the story we love finds us, invites us, pulls us into its world, and reveals God as the center of all life.

SEEING FRAGMENTS OF SALVATION

> The "fragments" that the preacher identifies as salvation experiences are to be found in the hope that emerges in the most hopeless of situations, the protest that rebels in the name of all that is human, and the persevering trust that clings to God even when God seems distant or absent . . . grounded in the resurrection of Jesus.[7]

In the hundred-year-old white pine stump from which that scrappy balsam springs, Larry and I see the shoot from the stump of Jesse. We see fragments of salvation in the disruption of the earth that will harden to make a path for the deer, in the crashing of lofty treetops as food is brought low for the lowly, and in the promise that, come another season, these scars on the earth will heal. Although nothing will ever be the same, life will return. Squirrels will play in the brush.

Ed and Peggy take me walking through the cemeteries. Ed paints a picture of Memorial Days before there were plastic containers and potted plants: cemeteries decorated with lilacs that had bloomed in backyards. He tells me about Ralph, the chief of police, his son Jackie, and their hairy little black and white dog who was deathly afraid of firecrackers. Peggy stops at the grave of her Grandpa Leanna and tells me how he had waited for her birth, how eager he was to see what she was going to be. That was the story Peggy's mother, Nancy, had always told her as they stood before this grave, whose markings reveal her grandpa's date of death—so nearly Peggy's birthday. I am no longer seeing gravestones; I am seeing fragments of salvation. The dead are raised.

It is almost Holy Cross Day, and one of those days I spend at the nursing home. The carts of evil-smelling laundry are trundling down the hallways, and I know that the flu is spreading like wildfire. I tell Lu Ann that I have been sent here to look for the Cross, and she describes where she's seen it lately. She had been wondering where she would find the patience and strength to change yet another bed without screaming. Leaning over her laundry cart, Lu Ann sees Marie, whose cross slips out of her uniform as she bends to help another resident. In that vision, Lu Ann finds her own world steadied.

Toward the end of our nursing home Bible study on the cross, Lina slowly negotiates her way among the wheelchairs and walkers, making her way into the circle. I see the strangest crucifix hanging around her neck. The cross is thin, and Jesus' body on it is even thinner. But the arms of the cross don't extend straight out. They're bending, carrying the weight of Jesus.

The Bible study group takes the fleshing stone to the text of this cross. They lament that this slender Jesus is carrying so much weight for them—weight that bends the arms of this cross. They scrape away at their sorrows, the load of their sin and the load of their guilts. They scrape at the pain and boredom and brokenness and losses of their lives—the what-ifs and the if-onlys that they can't stop thinking about. Helen squints to see a fragment of salvation:

> *That cross with the bent down arms reminds me of carrying my children. Not just when they were little babies, but also when they were bigger. They were getting heavy, but they'd want to come up. They'd stick out their little arms and look at me, and I'd take a deep breath, bend down, and lift them up. Maybe they wanted comfort, or reassurance, or they were hurting or scared. They were heavy, but I held them close. Jesus does that for us. That is why the cross's arms are bent.*

The sign "R-Place Bar and Grill" still hangs above the Genesee Street Clubhouse, where Lois works alongside adults with low living skills. "People still come in here looking for a brew," she says, "but now it's a place where people are reclaiming their lives." That's how she feels on a good day. On the day I come to set up our visit, she wonders if this will ever work. She struggles between the minefield of managed care and thin resources, and the apparent hopelessness of the situation of the clubhouse members. Later, seated around the table over coffee, the clients tell their stories of resurrection. One says that when she started coming to the clubhouse, recovering from drug addiction and mental illness, she couldn't remember how to fold a paper bag. She is grateful for those who have "stuck their arms out" to help. Lois and her coworkers listen with some surprise, as the clients express pride in slow progress and gratitude for companionship. Lois is coming to see things in a new way, she says. God is revealed as the center of all life:

> *Even when we are struggling, there is something holding us to that faith—even when we thought it was gone. We all feel helpless when people ask for help, and we can't take away the pain. But we can keep telling the good story of Jesus, so we can help people who need a lifeline. Sometimes, we may think we see things—like we think we see that this place is a bar. But it's not really a bar, it's the place people are reclaiming their lives. Maybe we can reclaim our world, too.*

Fragments of salvation: wherever the dead are raised and the poor receive good news.

LISTENING FOR THE ECHOES

Although our voices may not reverberate out in the world as they do when together we sing our favorite hymns inside the church, echoes of the gospel are everywhere. Together with those who know this landscape best, we sense these echoes of the gospel that are already reverberating in the marketplace, naming them as "grace" and amplifying them for those whose task it is to preach there.

The echoes of the gospel for which we are listening in the marketplace may reverberate in different ways:

- They may come to us when the story unfolds as it does in the scriptural story. But the story is made alive, *recast* for us today.
- They may echo in this new space to bring out something first seen and first heard, as the gospel is *recontextualized*.
- We may hear the gospel echo for us as new words, everyday words, or as a way of being disciples when the story is *translated* into our words and into deeds in the marketplace.
- Echoes of the scriptural story may be cast in the *fitting forms* and speech patterns of our local and contemporary culture.
- Something in the local landscape or architecture may echo the gospel *setting*.
- We may find ourselves and our familiar world, *reinterpreted* by the echoes in the story we hear in the marketplace.

RECASTINGS AND RECONTEXTUALIZATIONS

Recasting "keeps alive the simple forms of the tale" that not only "have to be there" but already are there as the road opens up for us through the biblical story and echoes through our own lives.[8] Like

Larry, when he suddenly stopped his bulldozer to announce the impending birth of a child. Or like Ray, as I discovered when I visited the Golden K (Kiwanis) Club and saw him conduct his first meeting as president.

Ray had told me that every third Wednesday, the meeting begins with "Name that Tune." I couldn't name any of the tunes. But, in all the refrains the Golden K's sang, I heard echoes of Jesus' experience of James' and John's reactions to his invitation to the way of the Cross. This morning, the morning after Ray's transfiguring installation banquet, the new president struggled to call the unruly group to order and failed resoundingly to attract anyone to volunteer to sell tickets at the old-time dance Friday night. After a dead silence, the group wound up again, announcing various other community happenings. Ray gaveled them to order, saying, "OK, but who's going to be able to sell tickets this Friday?" Again, silence. Then, a bevy of offers: to set up tables in the morning, to set up tables the day before, to do anything but sell tickets on Friday. Finally, Ray announced: "I'll be there to sell tickets at 6:30 Friday night. Who will join me?" Ray, servant and leader, took up his cross and invited those who would be "first" to follow him.

If recasting is keeping alive the simple forms of the tale, then recontextualization—setting the story in life lived in this space and time—brings out something that can make the old story "first heard." The new context lends new texture to the story, lifting up things we may never have considered before, things that are simply God's way of speaking to us today.[9]

This fresh Word became even clearer during my visit to the Mission Bible Training Center, a Bible-based substance-abuse rehabilitation center housed in an old ranch just outside of town. Jane had invited me for Bible study. Working their way through Genesis, the residents had come to the Jacob stories. That Esau would sell his birthright to Jacob for a bowl of lentil soup—no matter how hungry he might have been—had never seemed real to me until I heard this story in the company of people who had readily traded their birthrights and more for their next "high." Esau's experience suddenly had a new texture, a new depth, and his story was now available for me to know and tell.

It's hard to hear *anything* at the Buzz Saw, the coffee klatch of the Progressive Men of Caspian. But that's where Art introduced me to Tullio, so I could listen for gospel echoes in his stories about service to his country and what glory means to a veteran. Tullio, a World War II prisoner-of-war, talked about his capture, and his sense that he had not accomplished what he was supposed to because he had not laid down his life. He talked about glory in that context and about how someone could survive such an ordeal. Among the things that helped get him through were the Red Cross packages from folks back home.

Gary's stories had similar themes. He had watched his dad crawl on his knees toward the shrine of the Virgin of Guadelupe as an act of devotion and gratitude for his escape from his wartime captors. Gary's mother had been one of the women who went to work in the munitions plants, and she had lost a finger to the war effort. Gary recalled his own training to be a paratrooper in the 82nd Airborne during the Vietnam conflict. Through twists of fate, he was never called to serve in Vietnam, and it took him some time to get over the feeling that he, like Tullio, had somehow failed.

In this new context, the texture of Jesus' gift of freedom, the same reward, the same share of glory to all his disciples—came out in the story of James and John in Mark 10:25-45. Tullio's and Gary's sense of shame and loss brought out underlying issues of inadequacies and regrets. Their stories lifted up the stories of the glory of service, both on and behind the scene. The gospel echoes for us in the texture of our daily struggles. It frees us to believe and to tell one another that we are called simply to offer ourselves in faith that God, using us to God's liberating, gracious purpose, can make that offering meaningful. This is the way we lay down our lives. Visiting at the Buzz Saw infused this new meaning in an old story.

TRANSLATION AND FITTING FORMS

When we venture into the marketplace to listen for echoes of the gospel, we emulate the Luther of my childhood story: we are listening for the words we use to talk about bread—the ordinary stuff on which we spread peanut butter and jelly, the loaves we serve at our tables, the crusts for which we cry out in hunger and human need. When we talk about the Bread of Life, we know that it is of the ordinary stuff of our lives. This Bread is for us to share in common speech.

If Hilkert is right that the main preaching of the Christian community takes place in the sacred space of our ordinary daily lives and relationships, then we, as Sunday morning preachers will want to spend time in Monday's world, listening for the words we use in situations where we lose heart, betray, give up integrity, declare war and withhold amnesty, speak of love, foster hope, make commitments, grant forgiveness, take stands, and give witness. In these words we will find the echoes of the gospel. We will also want to listen for the packages—the patterns of communication, the culturally "fitting forms"—that take those words and make narratives, or stories, or ways of life for us in community. We will want to consider those forms, too, as the way the road opens for Jesus to come to us. James Neiman relates this to "knowing the 'songs'" of our listeners, the themes and variations of their lives, and "not being tone-deaf to them in the proclamation."[10]

We'll follow in the tradition of the writers of those two creation stories in Genesis. These stories use decidedly different rhythms of speech and express different relationships to the world around them. The two stories seem to be shaped for communities with two different sets of concerns about God and life together. In my two small communities in the Upper Peninsula of Michigan, our self-understanding, and the language we use to shape and communicate that self-understanding, is influenced by our Finnish, French-trapper, and Native American heritages. It is conditioned by our intimacy with nature, by our proximity to reservations and gambling casinos, by cable and satellite TV, by our work with the ill and frail and our work in the woods and the mill, by our memories of the mining culture and mining locations around which towns were settled, by the language of the school hallway and sporting events to which the whole community rallies, and by our agedness, geographic isolation, and harsh climate. We will expect to hear echoes of the gospel in these tongues and tones. Other communities will produce other tongues and tones.

In my communities probably the best time to listen is over morning coffee. One morning, I ran into Dan and Harmon, Harley-Davidson riding brothers in our neighborhood. Dan told me about their trips that summer, the people they had met, and their disgust that some bikers wouldn't ride with them. "Gold-Wingers don't ride with no Harley-Davidsons," the other bikers told them. Dan offered me his sermon for them: "Gold-Wingers, Harleys, what's the difference?" He lifted his "wings" and flashed his armpits as though he were out in the breeze. "We're all out here for the same reason, you know. To feel the wind blow in our faces, and to get the stink blown off of us!" That's Dan's translation, roughly, for the gospel of confession, forgiveness, and reconciliation that blows across the great—and small—divides of our lives.

At the café, you'll also discover that in our small towns, word-of-mouth news—gossip, perhaps—is the most natural and favored, if not fitting, form of communication. The noticing about our own and others' lives are peppered with information that we cull from our scanners, CB radios, the telephones, and TVs. We pass the news along using the peculiar speech common to these forums of the marketplace. Our conversation also carries echoes of the gospel as the form in which the good news of Jesus was spread from well to well, town to town, from Philip to Nathaniel.

Local jokes about our neighboring town of Covington made me wonder whether Nathaniel's quip "Can anything good come out of Nazareth?" might be the echo of ancient home town pride. Can anything good come out of Covington? My friend Kip tells jokes about our neighbors in the north:

> *They may have a gas station, but we have a gas station and a laundromat! Did you hear the one about the man who stopped in Covington to ask directions? He asked "Can I take this road to Amasa?" and the guy from Covington answered, "I don't care!" What do you get if you put LSD into kalamojakaa [fish head soup]? Answer: A trip to Covington!*

Another folk form for us, the Toivo-and-Eino stories, feature Toivo and Eino, as immigrants who never quite understand the culture of their new home in America. Toivo-and-Eino jokes are full of the stuff of human life. My husband told this one in an Easter sermon: Toivo and Eino come to America and are impressed with green, clear fields. Not a rock to be seen. Anywhere. So they bring all the relatives over to farm, declaring "It's wonderful! There are no rocks in America!" The relatives arrive, and when they begin to plow, they turn up rock after rock. Toivo and Eino just scratch their heads and say, "Boy what a funny country this is! The rocks here must grow upside down!"

Such fitting forms give us clues about the underlying message and concern and help us see where we're going, right from the start.[11] In my community, when we start with Toivo and Eino, we involve everyone in a joke, and although is it about us, a caricature offers us enough distance that we can laugh at the truth about ourselves. Being in on the joke from the start, we are drawn to hear and accept the echo of truth in the gospel story of the disciples, who like Toivo and Eino—are us but *not* us—gain some, but never quite enough, understanding of the new culture of the reign of God to get it right.

We may be surprised also to find liturgy as a common form of communication in the marketplace. Listening for echoes of the gospel and fitting forms in the story of the Unforgiving Servant, we discover that courtroom language is a rhythmic and responsive liturgy of confession and judgment:

> *"Do you understand, that if you plead guilty you give up certain rights? You give up the right to remain silent and not have that silence used against you. You give up the right to a jury of your peers and the right to take the stand to speak in your own defense. Do you understand this?" "Yes, your honor."*

The judge sometimes even takes time to deliver the sermon: "Don't apologize to me, apologize to your wife and kids, who will suffer from this drunk-driving conviction when you lose your job and your insurance rates go through the roof." Good judgment is a fitting form for a judge. But as I stopped and visited other workers in the courthouse, probation office, sheriff's office, and jail, the fitting forms I found were attitudes, demeanors, and patterns of professional matter-of-factness about the fallenness of the human predicament. These forms echoed nonjudgmental acceptance and compassion for neighbors who, for whatever reasons, found themselves in trouble with the law or needing the assistance of the judicial system. There is a place for such liturgy, too, in the sacred spaces and ordinary encounters of our lives. The marketplace preacher goes out to discover them already present in our work of God.

SETTINGS AND REINTERPRETATIONS

There is no substitute for going out with Larry and his friends to cruise the marketplace with a particular eye and ear attuned to the shape of the gospel. Out there, something we see will resonate, drawing our attention to the road opening its way out for us into the story of Jesus. Lu goes with me on a cemetery walk to discover what we believe about the resurrection and the life. And on the way down Cemetery Road, passing Cemetery Lake, she tells me that no one fishes this lake, swims this lake, boats this lake. Cemetery Lake is set apart from our other recreational lakes, and nothing happens there. But every fall, just before the ice lays the water to rest, the geese stop there on their way to a world beyond us. And every spring, as new life comes to our frozen wilderness, the geese will return, skidding across the opening waters. I am reminded that all of creation participates in this story, this hymn that is always being sung in the universe, waiting for us to hear its echoes, rhythms, and beats, waiting for us to join the song. Nature is reinterpreted for us in the text of our landscape as the sacred space it has always been: Holy to the Lord.

Our own creation, human culture, also opens the road. In part, it was the architectural style of the gambling casino—the vaulted ceilings and domes, and even the marble columns—that allowed for reinterpretation of the "Temple controversy." Is it lawful for a Christian to gamble? A snowmobile and a pickup truck, the current grand prizes, were set up on an "altar" in the center of the casino. Money changers and guards lined the walls. I was startled to see so clearly the echoes of the gospel story and its setting reinterpreted in light of our casino architecture. Discovery of the gospel story in the affairs of daily life reinterprets the story for us.

But the gospel story may reinterpret the affairs of daily life in startling ways as well. At the casino, the wheels of the one-armed bandits may be whirring and the coins may be tinkling in and out of the slots, but there is something about bringing echoes of the gospel into this setting with our bodily presence—the walking-talking-visible presence of the body of Christ—that opens up new possibilities for preaching in the church and in the world. And the gospel story may reinterpret us. Naming the sacredness of all commonspaces of our lives, offering a perspective on the economy of the whole of our lives as "holy to the Lord," reveals God as the center of all life in ways that may surprise us. What if our lives in the casino, too, are holy to the Lord? On the way home, Nancy (my gambling guide) and I talk about who God is for each of us. I realize that this is the first time the two of us have spoken together about God, the worth of our lives, and how we spend them.

Larry, cruising the parcel of land, looking for the road, tells me that his company has already put down $40,000 for the logging. I tentatively ask him whether he ever thinks about the land, and the animals that are displaced while he's working. I can tell that even this gingerly approached question surprises Larry, and makes him thoughtful. I can hear the echoes of $40,000 going "k-ching, k-ching" in the cash register of Larry's mind. Yet he is a small cog in that machinery. The economy Larry has more firmly in mind is more personal. He takes joy of making landings and skidways and opening the road in anticipation of the arrival of pickup trucks and loggers that mean harvest is underway. Everyone (me too) will get paychecks. We will be able to put bread on our tables. We are a community of loggers. Loggers cut down trees that will be made into things people need. And today, the bells of the last century's horses and Larry's Caterpillar bulldozer are inscribed "holy to the Lord." And the echo of the gospel is the tinkling of those bells sacred alongside the "k-ching, k-ching" of the marketplace's cash register. Playing the role of Preparer of the Road, readying the road for the timber harvest, and the road on which Jesus has come to meet us today, has reinterpreted Larry, offering another economy by which we can both judge the work of his life as a sacred vessel of God's presence.

But those of us who go out to hear and see must be prepared to come back reinterpreted by the text. Parish preachers may be changed in this encounter, as well as blessed.

I'd never been to a wrestling match. After hearing wrestling Coach Felger's John the Baptist premeet pep talk, I'd been thinking more about his having instructed the boys to keep "strong hands." He'd told me about the injury that had weakened one of his hands and ended his own wrestling career. When I went home, I rediscovered in the Old Testament lesson an injunction to Israel, "Do not fear, O Zion; let not let your hands grow weak" (Zephaniah 3:16). I wondered whether these words might be a wrestling reference. I decided to attend a meet to see and hear what echoes of the gospel would reinterpret this text for my community.

I didn't like watching the wrestling. The kids seemed to be in pain. It looked like it hurt. It looked like a fierce struggle—a life-and-death struggle. Struggle in which it was important not to fear, not to let your hands grow weak. As I took my seat in the bleachers, I realized that one of the wrestlers was a girl. Her presence in the competition made it even more difficult for me to separate this controlled situation—this sport—from violent struggle in real life. To me, it seemed as if this young woman was struggling against her male opponent to avoid being pinned down and raped. I didn't want him to handle her like that. The crowd watched with horror tinged with excitement. This girl did not let her hands grow weak. When she finally pinned her opponent, the spectators went wild. A place in my heart rejoiced in her strength and her will to wrestle. I believed she had a right to compete. At the same time, I had a strong sense that she never should have allowed herself to be in such a position—literally, on all fours, waiting for this boy to grab her under the breasts from behind. The boy who had been beaten was thoroughly humiliated, fighting tears. Then I was angry that he had been put in this situation. I wondered whether he'd held back, afraid of any number of things. The girl's third opponent did, I believe, hold back. The men had shouted at him, time and time again, to "get between her legs!", but he wouldn't. He won anyway.

I had gone to the meet hoping to have the biblical text about weak hands recast, recontextualized, and reinterpreted in the marketplace. And I had found myself reinterpreted by the text and the marketplace, wondering whether this is how my preaching is experienced, wrestling with newly realized ambivalence about being a woman who is a preacher and making myself available to be the Word's body.[12] Perhaps this is how all of us find ourselves—unlikely opponents in an unlikely interface with God's Word, unexpected observers and translators of daily life into God's life, life in God. Uncomfortable in this position amidst conflicting expectations. Yet offering ourselves, engaging in the struggle, not letting our hands grow weak. "It is only after interpreters have been interpreted by the text can they become preachers," Lucy Rose acknowledges.[13] So maybe Larry and I are finally getting ready to preach.

LIVING ON THE INTERFACE

Neither the text of Scripture nor the text of the marketplace and our bodily lives within the marketplace is a passive participant. Both have life within the lively space of our fleshly interface, and each has a will of its own. We wouldn't expect less from any space that God has graced, that God has named as the arena of God's activity. Like the Luther in my story, by venturing into the marketplace we expose ourselves to both risk and joy. I have found joy in breaking out of the drafty castle into the colorful, happening world in which the hearers of my sermons must preach. I have found joy squinting into the viewfinder with them and seeing fragments of salvation, tramping around with them, listening for echoes of the gospel story in which we all long to live.

For the most part, the visits that comprised my foray into the marketplace were the best visits of my life. The Word around which these visits gathered us creates an opportunity, an intimacy, a community, an excuse to discover something about God together. Sometimes naming the grace we had discovered invited us to pray together, newly mindful that all people and things are vessels of God's sacred presence. Sometimes the welcome was warm. People seemed to have been waiting to talk about the questions that nobody ever addresses but that are the real places in their lives into which they have always hoped the gospel would crash. The world, the marketplace, also grew curious about the story we brought into it. We saw people looking over the fence just as the little boy watched our outdoor worship and wondered we were up to. We were creating interest for the classic text.

But there is also risk. The world doesn't always like the church to leave its castle. "Who's taking care of the church?" three-year-old Travis asked, frightened when I came to visit him in the hospital. Some people see us as tenders of the sacred fires, and if it appears that we're not "in there" protecting them, how can people rest easy in their work in the world?

We may need to renegotiate our understandings of ourselves and our relationships with our parishioners and the community, making mutual adjustments, in the interface where grace is named. It's hard to be in the real world and maintain illusions that the preacher is not quite real. One day, reaching for a frozen pizza at the grocery store, I caught a woman staring at me. When I met her eye she blurted out, "Well, I guess *you* have to eat, too." A pastor can't be anything but flesh and blood, out in the concrete reality of the marketplace, but my seminary courses never covered the protocol of going gambling with our members. I'd invited Nancy to go gambling. Did that mean I should provide her gambling stake? (I settled for buying her lunch.) Nancy had to work it out, too. What did it mean to take her pastor gambling? What if the pastor lost? What if she *won*? (Nancy settled for letting me play only nickels and quarters, and she demonstrated the dollar machines and her gift for blackjack.)

Because for so long we've pretended that we can keep God and our lives separate, it's just scary for some people to see the church in the world. When the preacher and those who are with her squinting into the viewfinder are intent on revealing God as the center of all life, things can become uncomfortable. People don't want their pastor to find them in the casino. Anyone who can continue to believe that there are spaces that are not "holy to the Lord," doesn't have to watch his language and "act nice" all the time.

This push and pull between welcoming acceptance and distance, dismissal, or even removal from the world of everyday life, may be preparing us for preaching. Rebecca Chopp recalls Jesus' own such experience in his hometown (Luke 4) and the reality that proclamation begins in the "caughtness" between fulfillment and rejection.[14] This caughtness is finally a tension that Dow Edgerton names for preacher-interpreters who "must live in a self-conscious way on the margin, at a place where boundaries meet."[15] This tension propels us toward the creative moment that brings an authentic sermon into being.

⌖

Larry and I have braved the elements. I get out of the car while he digs out his camera. He never knows what he's going to see out there. This time it's his pastor on his bulldozer. I am excited to have this remarkable experience recorded for posterity, but my feet are cold. In fact, I am chilled to the bone. When I return home, I huddle by a radiator, hugging a hot cup of tea. I jot down a few notes about what I heard and what I saw when I was bulldozing with Larry. Tomorrow is Friday, sermon-writing day, but right now I am bushed from keeping loggers' hours, overcome with the richness of the gift Larry has shared with me: a day which has been inscribed "holy to the Lord." I am warming up.

NOTES

1. Rose, *Sharing the Word*, 63. Rose points out that this understanding of the Word of God as not restricted to the Bible is not a new idea. It shares with traditional theology the claim that the Word is operative in creation, history, and nature. She cites Charles Rice, who asserts that the Word "happens" in the world, breaking out in cultural forms, in art, in human nature, and in the preacher's own humanity, as the Word again becomes flesh.

2. Diehl, *The Monday Connection*, 31.

3. Lueking, *Preaching*, 6.

4. Thulin, *The "I" of the Sermon*, 16–17.

5. Hilkert, *Naming Grace*, 184.

6. *Ibid.*, 193. Hilkert defines naming grace as "'naming the present,' trying to identify where the Spirit of God is active in contemporary human life and in communities of believers who make the gospel a

concrete reality in limited and fragmentary, but still tangible ways." She borrows the term "fragments of salvation" from the work of Edward Schillebeeckx.

7. *Ibid.*, 36.

8. Byatt, *Possession*, 379.

9. Hilkert, 49. "Reflection on culture, people's lives, and human experience is necessary not merely to make a homily relevant, but to hear God's Word today."

10. Nieman, *"Preaching People Out of Church,"* 111.

11. Long, *Preaching and the Literary Forms of the Bible*, 16. Long addresses the need hearers have to be "clued in," or prepared to listen in a certain way. Fitting forms for the community have a capacity to send these signals.

12. Bozarth, *The Word's Body*, 52. "The text is not re-created, but the interpreter accepts its givenness and continues its creation . . . by allowing the text's potential to become realized in the availability of his or her own bodily presence."

13. Rose, 68.

14. Chopp, *The Power to Speak*, 70.

15. Edgerton, *The Passion of Interpretation*, 66

Habakkuk the Channel Surfer Meets God's Billboards: Rob and Lois

Oh Lord, . . . Why do you make me watch terrible injustice? Why do you allow violence, lawlessness, crime and cruelty to spread everywhere? (Habakkuk: 1:1–4; 2:1–4)

The apostles said to the Lord, "Increase our faith!" (Luke 17:5–10)

Habakkuk reached for the channel changer after watching about a half hour of the Clinton video. "Why," he muttered to himself in disgust, "are we being forced to watch this?"

But as Habakkuk surfed the channels his despair only grew. Kosovo. JonBenet Ramsey. School shootings. The breakdown of the family. Y2K and the end of the world as we know it. Even The Weather Channel was showing endless footage of raging hurricanes, rising floodwaters, people fleeing, homes being swept away, El Niño, global warming.

The local news made him feel just as helpless—another plant closing, the latest wrangling at some board meeting, a drunk-driving fatality.

Habakkuk forgot that he couldn't fast-forward through the commercials that push him relentlessly to buy stuff, eat stuff. Budweiser, Nike, Burger King, *now* . . . even prescription drugs for afflictions he didn't suffer from. But there was no cure for what was ailing the world.

Finally, Habakkuk found a sitcom and thought maybe he could just escape into laughter. But after five minutes and ten crude and tasteless references to body parts and bodily functions, he quit and went to bed.

Lying in the dark, the prophet Habakkuk couldn't quite turn it all off. The horrors of disaster and starvation. The pettiness of people's lives. Some nights he even wondered whether there really is a God. Violence, destruction, strife, hunger, and injustice seem to have the upper hand. Other nights he spent crying out to God to do *something*! "Why, God, do you make us look at these things that we can't do anything about? How long must we cry out for help, for you to do something?"

"*You* do this," the Lord answers Habakkuk. "Write a word, as big as a billboard, so that even those running from the violence and destruction can read it as they tear madly down the streets. It is a word that will speak of God's purpose for the end, when life will prevail over the forces of evil. Wait for it. It is coming at the ripe time, in God's time. So no matter how long it takes, it will be right on time. The righteous will live by this faith."

"Increase our faith!" the disciples cry out years later. They are gazing straight at the Word that God sent at just the right time. They are walking with Jesus, the billboard that—in Jesus' violent, unjust death on the Cross, and in his victorious resurrection on Easter day—shows us that God lives, God rules. But that plan is still unfolding for these disciples, as God's plan for the world still unfolds for us in the promise that at the right time, Christ will come again to draw this whole mixed bag of a world to himself.

In the meantime, "Increase our faith!" We need faith to rear our children, and pass on the faith. We need faith to face the future and stand fast in the midst of violence. We need faith to speak the truth to one another in love; we need faith to forgive; we need faith to raise a billboard of the good news of God's rule in Jesus for a world that is running, escaping, and fleeing in terror from violence. Increase our faith, we pray!

But Jesus says that we have what we need, that *more* is not the answer. He tells a story about plowing and the ordinary hard work of just tending to sheep. He tells a story about putting on an apron and preparing dinner. About thankless slave labor. Hard work, sure, but not save-the-world work. Is it possible that *God* has already saved the world? That we just have to do what's put before us, the work of ordinary, everyday life? That we don't have to understand God's plan exactly, but have faith enough to leave the big picture to God?

We all feel helpless when someone asks us for help that seems beyond our resources. When someone we love is in pain that we can't fix. When the problems of the world are too big for us to sort out. But what if we, who are baptized into Christ's death and resurrection, bearing the Cross of Christ marked on our foreheads like a sign of God's hope for the future, are being called upon only to keep telling the story of God's love for us in Jesus? What if it's up to us to tell the people who are running right by us? What if, by our faithful work in the places where God has already called us, we point people not to our own resources or strength to fix everything but to our confidence in God's love for us and the world in sending Jesus to be our Savior?

Rich likes coming to church, he says, because he knows that if his three-year-old daughter Toni Lu should run screaming down the aisle after the sermon, someone, *someone* is going to reach out and stop her before she runs outside and into the road. Other places, he says, he can imagine people just watching her, raising their eyebrows not lifting a finger to stop her and saying, "Huh! Where are her parents? Why aren't they watching her? Parents these days!"

Rich's story tells us something about what it means to be a family of faith not only in our churches but also out in the world. It is true that most people see the world's overwhelming problems—violence, poverty, lack of time for anyone to listen, alcohol and drugs addiction, and abuse of women and children—as being the responsibility of someone else. "Where are their parents?" Or, "Why isn't someone doing something about this?" We fold our arms against our chests, cluck about what this world is coming to, and stand by as people run screaming toward disaster.

But what if all we're called to do in faith is to stick out our arms to keep people from running into the traffic? What if, right where we are, we can be the body of Christ, the arms of Christ, saving the world by being a billboard, a sign for God's saving grace?

Rob Willman, our high school's at-risk coordinator, has taken time to talk with me about the challenges that face both teachers and students in our world today. Our kids don't have to pass through metal detectors or weapons searches when they walk into school. Not yet. But both students and teachers say that the "Drug Free Zone" signs posted outside are the school's biggest joke. The rules of the so-called drug-free environment are enforced sporadically, applied unjustly, and are interpreted on the basis of who's who. And no one has the answers.

Rob concedes that put that way, the problems are too big for him to address. So the way he looks at it, drugs and alcohol abuse are not the problem: they are symptoms of an emptiness, a space that is not being filled with the love and acceptance everyone needs. It's not a problem only for kids, he says. We all look for and need love and when we can't find it, we either escape through drugs and alcohol, excessive sleep, food, sex, or work, or we strike out in violence and anger. Kids are just looking to fit in, he says. We all are. We are all hungry for recognition, for someone who is happy to see us. Everyone wants to belong and feel important, to be part of some kind of a family, to know something of the kind of unconditional love God holds for us.

But Rob feels that he can do something to help. He can look kids in the eye and know their names. Stick an arm out if they're about to run into traffic, or be there for those who have been hurt. He can't save or fix them or the society, but he can love them and be there. He can help them move beyond anger at the injustices. He can help them make life productive and meaningful.

Rob sees kids helping one another. He sees them sticking out an arm. They don't always wait for some adult or an authority to do something. He's seen hope for the future: when someone was running by, somebody, the closest person, just reached out, and the person in trouble knew they were loved by someone. Rob keeps the faith, he says, by holding on to God's plan for him, whatever it is, doing what he can each day.

We're not all working in the breach like Rob. But he points to some amazingly everyday ways we can make a difference. Learn someone's name. Look that someone in the eye. Fill up empty spaces with affirmation. We are all in a position, sometimes, to stick out an arm, not wait for someone else, someone more responsible, to do it.

We don't have to save the world. But how possible it might be just to point people, one at a time, to God's saving grace in Jesus. What a wonderful image: Think of us, as people of faith, out in the world sticking out our arms as people run by fleeing violence and destruction. We, with our outstretched arms, can be signs of God's kingdom come. God's future, the victory over the dehumanizing forces of evil, is already springing up where in faith we stick out our arms.

Right on Genesee Street, we can see another sign of the world's being reclaimed for God.

The old sign, R-Place Bar and Grill, still swings above the street, but new lettering on the door reads, "Genesee Street Clubhouse." Old-timers will tell you that the R-Place had a reputation. And every once in a while, Lois tells me, someone still stumbles in hoping for a brew. But she also tells me that R-Place has been reclaimed for God as holy space, as a place where lives are reclaimed and brew is not what they serve up anymore.

If you walk in now, you'll be welcomed warmly by the clubhouse members, who are part of a special program for adults with low daily-living skills. You'll remember we met some of these folks last year at the Beef-a-Roo restaurant. But now, instead of just going out for coffee, they are learning how to make coffee for themselves and to offer a cup to a guest. They talk with pride of learning to sell snacks to each other, to clean a bathroom, to publish a newsletter, to follow the steps for making franks and beans, to do dishes, to take phone calls and messages. They are proud of their clubhouse. One of the women turns on the old neon lights to the bar, and in its glow, she tells me how she is struggling to find her way back from drug and alcohol addiction and mental illness.

"When I started my recovery, I couldn't fold a paper bag. I couldn't remember how to do it." She's proud of the things she's been able to reclaim for herself, and she's grateful for the people who have stuck their arms out to help her recover her life in simple ways. It makes a difference, other members will tell you, just to have someplace to be. "People understand us here," they say. "We can try something." "When I need to talk, there are people here." Like "our" Lois Maki, they say.

But "their" Lois Maki will tell you this isn't save-the-world stuff. It's just her work, to lend an arm or a hand. Picking the pizza crust up off the floor. It's the work any parent knows. It's hard work. Put-on-an-apron work. Tend-the-sheep work. At 2:30 P.M., she has to turn her flock over to God or others for safekeeping, having done what she could that day. But bit by bit, one person at a time, such work changes lives—and maybe the world.

If we were looking for a sign, for a Word from the Lord, we might see one at the old R-Place. We glimpse the inbreaking of God's future now, the new life and victory over evil and suffering that is promised in Jesus' resurrection from the dead. It's not beyond us.

Habakkuk, Rich, Rob, and Lois show us how to keep the faith while we wait for Jesus' coming. We have the help of the Spirit—the Spirit of the risen Christ given to us in our baptisms so that we can live out this resurrection in our daily work. This is the Spirit that can rekindle and light a fire under the faith that is in us, so we are able to stick out our arms to those who run by us in fear and confusion. We are not able to save the world, but we are here to announce God's love and salvation for the world one person at a time.

Today Lance, Gloria, and Ricky join Habakkuk, Rich, Rob, Lois, and all of us in this extraordinary, ordinary life we share in Christ's body. Drowning and rising in the waters of baptism, they too join the labor of those who know the world has already been saved by Jesus. Filled with the Spirit of Jesus, they can rest with us in hope and some peace and confidence that what they do is enough for the day.

That Spirit can teach us to pray every day:

Lord, I don't need faith to move mountains. Lord knows, there are bulldozers and dynamite enough around here for that. But, Lord, just breathe on me, stir up my faith, to move me. Amen.

Chapter 3

I'm in the Picture, Too:
Being One Who Names Grace

There is another way of saying this. Aim for the chopping block. If you aim for the wood, you will have nothing. Aim past the wood, aim through the wood; aim for the chopping block.
—Annie Dillard, *The Writing Life*

Baz Luhrmann's seductive multimedia vulgarization of Romeo and Juliet is intended to convince the short-attention-span generation that the Bard is one dead white male whose observations about human behavior are as topical now as when they were made 400 years ago. The result is an interpretation . . . filled with tattoos, shoulder holsters, leather jackets, Hawaiian shirts, earrings, sex, drugs and rock 'n' roll. . . . It is clear that Luhrmann . . . is using familiar imagery to create a non-verbal comfort zone for a contemporary audience whose patience might be severely tested by period dialogue.
—Duane Dudek, review of *William Shakespeare's 'Romeo & Juliet,'* by Baz Luhrmann, *Milwaukee Journal-Sentinel*

"The kingdom of heaven is like treasure hidden in a field. . . . Again, the kingdom of heaven is like a merchant in search of fine pearls. . . . Again, the kingdom of heaven is like a net which was thrown into the sea and gathered fish of every kind. . . . Have you understood all this?" They said to him, "Yes." And Jesus said to them, "Therefore every scribe which has been trained for the kingdom of heaven is like a householder who brings out of his treasure what is new and what is old."
—from Matthew 13, *RSV*

Larry dug the camera out of the glove compartment. I took up my pose over by the bulldozer. My smile was becoming as frozen as the rest of me while Larry squinted into the viewfinder. I was thinking that maybe he was a little too far back to get a really good picture of me anyway, and I almost suggested he move in a little closer. But in the split second before I could say anything, Larry was able to tell me how not only the picture, but also the day, would be framed for him forever: "I'm trying to get our road in . . . there it is!" And finally he snaps it.

Larry's picture isn't really a picture of me. He aims his shot through me, toward the road we have made together. Again, he is teaching me about preaching, about the gift of focus that can reveal God—not ourselves, but through our selves—as the center of all life.

Annie Dillard offers another way of saying this: Aim for the chopping block, not for the wood. She paints a hilarious picture of herself writing in a Puget Sound cabin and learning to chop firewood. She whacks and hacks away with great effort, producing tiny chips, and entertaining the true wood-splitting islanders who gather to watch. Then one night, in a dream, in a vision, she is given to understand the difference between chopping at wood and splitting logs cleanly: you aim for the chopping block. Aim past the wood; aim through the wood; aim for the chopping block.

Larry, of course, is an accomplished woodsman. He already knows this. He knows enough to aim his shot right past me, right through me. Aiming for the road, he is shooting for Jesus. This picture is my sun chart. It checks my preaching compass against any magnetic distortions of reality under my feet as I begin to plot the way of the sermon through high ground and swamp. In this vision, Larry serves as the Holy Spirit, truing my aim.

❀

Larry's picture frames our road. But I am in this picture too. Even though God is truly the center, and even though I am a little smaller than I thought I'd be, I am in the middle of it. I am in the picture as Larry's pastor. This squinting into the viewfinder takes time and a discerning eye. This aim-taking on Word and World that becomes a sermon for a gathered community takes practice and dexterity. If I aim at the text, I will have nothing.[1] How do I avoid hacking away with great effort, producing only chips that warm no one else? What words, what narratives, what patterns of speech will I use to split logs and open worlds, to aim through the text and open it along the grain of our lives to discover Jesus there?

Those who have cruised, blazed, and taken the fleshing stone to the stories we hold in common now help me take aim to find the "simple, clean forms of the tale that must be there,"[2] splitting its world open so the gathered community can step through it into the story we love. There we discover Jesus already stepping into our world, the world God has so loved.

Fragments of salvation have been gathered, and already the gospel has been heard echoing throughout that world. Now, as the parish preacher, I lay it all out and comb through it, looking for the sermon that has always been there. I go through it searching as though for treasure, hidden in the field. I discern for it like a merchant sizing up fine pearls. I have cast a wide net and it is teeming with fish. As a scribe trained for the kingdom of heaven, like a householder, I look for the thing that makes "all these things seem first seen."[3] It finds me. And I go looking for it. Then I take aim, not for the wood of the pews but through the people who sit in them toward the doors opening into the world. I aim not to transform the congregation—I aim in such way that "the whole Christian community aims to transform society."[4] I aim to reveal the world in which the sermon must live as the place where God already dwells with us, offering the marketplace a vision of itself as graced, offering it the possibility of living in a new economy.

Having cruised the text and driven behind the plowblade with Larry, who teases out rocks more by feel than by sight, who opens landings and makes skidways for the harvest and the pickup trucks as solitude gives way to the picnic in the wilderness, I find it less scary that I now have an ax in my hand. But it is Friday, and the ax is in my hand. I am in the picture too.

THE GAP

Larry takes a step back, and to include the road in the picture, he does not get me in a close-up. He puts a little distance between us, and he shows me something I am looking for.

Try as I might to eliminate the otherness between preacher and congregation as together we crowd around the viewfinder, as much as our relationship has been renegotiated and become more real out there where the sermon has to live, I can't quite close this gap.[5] And I'm not sure I want to. I'm not sure that being set apart and living within a partnership of equals in a roundtable church isn't a desirable and livable paradox, an enlivening and dynamic tension.[6] The gap between the merchant and the pearl that the merchant seeks is what makes for an interesting search. It is the perceived gap between dirt and treasure, the unlikely connections between fields, pearls, and fish, that illuminates the realm of God. It is the friction of interaction and then the gap, the space into which sparks fly and catch, that makes ignition and combustion possible. Just as Larry graces our community with his day-by-day competency in road building, the professional preacher brings gifts and skills that bear fruit for the life of the household of faith.[7]

After all, the Luther of my story goes to the marketplace, but he remains quite conscious that he is there as an observer with a particular task. Eventually, he returns alone to the castle with the common words for the bread of the table and the bread of the beggar, and he joins them to the Bread of Life. The Luther of the historical story has dinner with all the best scholars and linguists, discusses the ins and outs of his translation, and produces a work that brings coherence to a vernacular, links the vocabulary for faith and life, and provides a common tongue for his people.[8] There is a gathering around Luther's table; there is the peopled landscape of the marketplace. But come Friday morning, back in the castle, it is Luther who takes aim. This is his work of God, and this is God's gift for the world, not himself, but through his self, for us.

Raised with a grammar of hierarchies and dualisms, we find it difficult to put a name to this creative, collaborative commonspace located on the fluid interface between the gospel and the world. In our confusion over changing roles and shifting boundaries, we may find ourselves like the seminarian who sincerely recounted one of the joys of the preaching life as "sitting at the head of the roundtable." We may not have the words for this way of being, but with such a sharp and powerful instrument in our hands, with such an ambivalent and ambiguous history of doing good and doing violence, it is critical to know who we are. It's crucial to know where we're aiming—out the door—and for what we're aiming—to open certain worlds, to reveal certain roads, and to capture Jesus there. We find ourselves in this multiverse fumbling for a language of authority for ourselves as preachers under which we might dare both to raise an ax to rend and split open worlds, and to aim and desire just as powerfully to mend and link worlds. In other words, we aim to *cleave*.

THE OUTSIDER WITH THE LISTENING HEART

As Sunday morning preachers, we are in the picture. We are smaller than we thought would be, but we are right in the middle, even if God is at the center. Claiming the gift of set-apartness for creative and lively collaboration at the roundtable, bringing to bear the life-giving power to cleave as trained scribes or householders, might just be possible if we have listened deeply as outsiders for the underlying issues of our communities. It might just be possible if we have cultivated what Robert Schreiter calls a listening heart for the insider voices and a reverence for the ways God is already present in this interface, for the ways the text has already gotten a life.[9]

I was standing in the cemetery with Ed and Peggy when the question of what the outsider can offer suddenly assumed a special poignancy and urgency. In the cemetery, where we bring our most profound questions and where absence screams louder than presence, the heart must listen most deeply. The cemetery is the commonspace of the landscape of grief, love, and honored past for our community, but unlike Ed, Peggy, and most of the congregation, I am not connected to this small city of the dead by blood and blessed memory. I am an outsider here.[10]

Taking the fleshing stone to Job's cry that a monument to his life's story should remain after his death, and scraping away at our experience of grief and questions about family life in the resurrection, we have come up with answers from within our culture that fail to assure, clothe, or warm us. Our cemeteries leave us cold. The popular understandings of heaven as a biological family reunion—without the fighting—still leave us unbearably separated now. And Jesus' words about what it will mean to be children of the resurrection seem to take even that hope away, and they leave us with . . .what?

The preaching group has asked me what I believe and how as their pastor, I can stand up to all the sorrows they bring. They ask me point-blank, trustful and expectant that I can bring an answer to their ache, looking to me to help them connect to a larger city of the living, a larger, more hopeful reality they are sure I know.[11] They are looking for worlds to be laid open and mended, for the dead to be raised, for me to squint into the viewfinder with them until they can see the road on which Jesus and the saints in light—no, not the saints in light, but Brad, Ellen, and Renja—will come to meet them so we can be whole again. They step back and count on my distance for this moment, hoping that when they can't see for the tears, I will show them something they are looking for. I tell them what I believe: that we meet now in the Eucharist, that all the baptized will be family in a way that multiplies our joy and reunion at the marriage feast that knows no end. But this answer comes to them in a foreign tongue, from too great a distance, and it fails to satisfy, fails to connect.

It is Thursday, and I wonder what to make of the group's desire for the sermon:

> *to reassure the members that there is a heaven where we will be reunited with our loved ones. . to show us through cemetery visits how we connect with one another in our common grief, and how we connect with our loved ones in a physical way. . .*

and I wonder what to make of Jesus' words in the gospel lesson for the day:

> Those who belong to this age marry and are given in marriage;
> but those who are considered worthy of a place . . . in the
> resurrection of the dead neither marry nor are given in marriage
> . . . and are children of God, being children of the resurrection.
> (Luke 20:34-36)

I wonder what to make of what I have seen and heard in the cemetery with Ed and Peggy. What to make of the family nature of plots,
their boundaries, and the careful decisions about who rests with whom
in the ground? What to make of the segregation by religious community? Or the lengths to which the grieving have gone to provide
grave markers, even crafting them out of cedar posts or laboriously
pounding tin in days of scarcity; or the lengths to which some parents
have gone to remember an infant, long-dead, whom they barely knew,
whose life was tragically cut short back in those dreadful years before
penicillin? What to make of the old cemetery's angels, lambs, and gates
swinging into eternal sunshine? And the new plots' personalized mar-
bles depicting cherished camps, an open Bible, a ten-point buck, an
Old Style stein, a country church, or a logging skidder?

I wonder what to make of Ed's parting words, asking me not to mention his remembrance of a teacher as lazy or the pathos of a neighbor who drowned himself for sorrow after the death of his wife.
Recognizing the taboos, but moved by Ed's expression of the very
hopelessness and embodied reality of the grief into which I aim to
prepare a road for Jesus to meet us, I ask: "Why not?" "Everyone has
a story," Ed explains, "but not all stories are meant to be told." Those
stories were for me, he says, they are "not a stories to be told in
church." They are not mine to appropriate for my own ends.[12]

I wonder, though, what is the difference between private, intimate
speech and public, corporate speech? What is the difference between
what Ed and I talk about in the place the sermon has to live and the
words I will use from the pulpit as our spokesperson when the community gathers?[13] Does it make a difference that when Ed and I talk,
we can have a direct exchange, a give-and-take, and that either one
of us can leave the conversation if it becomes too intense? What are
our options in corporate or communal speech? What are the stories

that cannot be told? What are the stories that we cannot tell in church?[14] When *must* we tell them precisely there? When are we who are trained to cleave worlds called upon to offer stories that give voice to the unspeakable, to that which has been silenced or that which we ourselves have been unable to name?[15] If we are to be powerful namers of grace, if we are to tell the truth that the shape of our baptized lives is death and resurrection, and if that crucified and risen One is to come to meet us, must we not also be unflinching articulators of evil?

Squinting into this viewfinder, I wonder: How were the dead raised in what I'd seen and what I'd heard and had been told in the cemetery not to say about family, our past, death, life, love, and loss? How could I, as an outsider, aim to give us something to cleave to? How could what we believe be lifted into contrast and coherence with gospel culture and tradition in a way that would split open this world of grief for us? How could it be told in an insider's tongue that would reveal God as the center of all life, as the God not of the dead but of the living, in a way that makes us whole?

It is only Thursday. I suspend panic, allowing my heart to listen beyond its own beat. I visit Brian and Joe, our funeral directors. I tell them what I've seen and heard in the cemeteries, and I ask what they've seen and heard as they've stood there with the families of our communities. How do we folks here name the grace of resurrection in the midst of our grief?

Brian and Joe have never been asked these questions, so we have coffee. They talk with me for an hour about the faith and strength they need for their work. We talk about what they believe, about what we believe, about the resurrection of the dead. They, too, start squinting into the viewfinder, finding the road and seeing how the dead come to be raised by the One who meets us there. This, they suggest, is the echo of the gospel in the cemetery, the fragment of salvation we are meant to grasp there:

☙ Life matters

☙ Love never dies

⚘ Our new continuing, but different, relationships with those
who have died may be preparing us for our new relationships
with one another in the life to come

And then it is Friday, so I aim for this chopping block, and not at the
wood of the text. With this is mind, I struggle to let go of my own need
for the congregation to "get" the nuances of the Job and Lukan texts
and my need to "correct" their human and traditional understandings
of the continuing bonds of love and relationship that are both severed
in death and resumed by eternal life. I work instead toward an empow-
ering transformation of this understanding that is reassuring in its refor-
mulation and usable by the community for its own proclamation.[16]

I connect the stories that Peggy told me when we visited the Amasa
cemetery—stories about her date there with her husband-to-be, about
her Grandpa Leanna, her first occasion of sin, and the sacred, set-apart
space of the cemetery. I connect the stories with fitting forms of
humor, because these are Peggy's stories, and this is Amasa. Like most
oral cultures, our Amasa community enjoys humor as its most fitting
form for opening us up to hard truths. Peggy is really a product of this
culture and enjoys telling stories on herself. Peggy's stories are already
funny, so they pretty much determine that humor will shape their
telling. The community knows she has lost a younger brother, so her
cemetery humor is not seen as trivializing or disrespectful.

For Ed's community, I connect the stories Ed has told me about
Ralph, the lilacs, the little dog who was afraid of firecrackers, with
the names of our departed congregational pillars who rest in the
Stambaugh cemetery. I connect the stories using the fitting forms of
genealogy, because these are Ed's stories, and this is Stambaugh. In
Stambaugh, the old is passing away, and the new isn't in easy conti-
nuity with the ethnic and social heritage that founded this church.
Ed was the town's grocer for many years, and he holds many of the
stories of our community's past. In this time of transition, we are challenged to find ways to honor and remember—but not enshrine—the
past. Lifting up the names of the faithful who have gone before us is
a fitting form of genealogy that enriches our new life together by
telling us the important story of our origins.

In both versions, I connect the stories of the two congregations through the grave of a common ancestor in the faith. I connect them with our group members' desires to see the ways our connections endure; the ways in which the stories of those who have gone before us are alive and available to strengthen our faith until we are reunited in the new life to come.

I connect these stories of our time with the story of Job, the anguish of the ages, and with his desire for a lasting memorial that would testify to his struggle. I connect them with the picture Jesus paints for the faithful of every time—eternal life as children of God, children of the resurrection. I connect these stories to the everyday words and aphorisms Brian and Joe have shared with me. Their words connect our stories to the story of the life of faith. My listening heart remembers the words Mel had delivered in the quiet that followed Rich's anguished plea for some guarantee to which he could cleave. And then I take aim through all these words and stories toward Mel's and Jesus' proclamation of hope and promise: "For to God, all of them are alive."

Lois reflects on the tension and fluidity of whose story this is, whose gift is this sermon-product, what I, the preacher, who takes aim as an outsider with a listening heart can contribute: "You took what we said and shared with one another. You connected all our stories and feelings and made them beautiful. Then you took what we did, and you gave it to our congregations for us."[17]

It is up to Lois and her friends to decide whether the result enhances the community's understanding and whether this expression of faith makes a difference in people's lives.[18] After the sermon, in qualified acceptance of this new way of looking at life and death, Rich tells me, "I now understand: in heaven you are supposed to be with your loved ones, except it's different. I hope it's similar." Some people said that they felt that they would now even be able to comfort others with this news: "I think I'd be able to explain to someone what heaven might be like, and how we would all know each other." "I would be able to tell others that yes, Jesus is with us even in death, and I could give clear pictures of this connection even in the cemetery."

I'm in the picture, too. I am a namer of grace, and I have powerful tools to bring to bear in this naming. But now I know that I'm not the only namer of grace, and I will wield my ax and aim differently on Fridays because I know this.

It is another week now, and the lessons are about Eli and his role in Samuel's awakening to God's voice (I Samuel 13), and Philip's invitation to Nathaniel to come and meet the Messiah (John 1:43-51). I've been sent to sit with people around the commonspace of their kitchen tables, and I've asked, "Who brought you closer to Jesus? Who has helped you know God's voice?"

The stories I've heard have revealed people as good namers of the grace in their lives—if only someone asks. At these tables, I've heard stories of prayer groups and spouses, friends' mothers who taught bedtime prayers on sleep overs, and former pastors who sparked and confirmed. These stories of faith mentors ring clear for me.

But then I ask Lily who had brought her closer to Jesus. First she names her husband, Arvo, and I happily write his name in the spouse column. She credits Arvo with bringing her to church when their only vehicle was the dump truck. I stop writing and look at Lily. She sees where I'm going. She reminds me that "it wasn't like it is now," when utility vehicles impart status and cars are for people who can't afford to spend so much. I still wait for the connection: how did this experience bring Lily closer to Jesus? But that is the end of her story.

Instead, she tells me another story—a story about her daughter Dulcie. I write her name in the children column. One Sunday, during the sermon, Dulcie had fallen asleep on Lily's lap. Glancing down, Lily was horrified to see that Dulcie's hair had become wound around the little buttons on Lily's bodice. Lily was certain that Dulcie would feel her hair caught, wake up, and start screaming. And then, of course, all the crabby old ladies in church would shush Dulcie and disapprove of Lily. Lily concludes her story: Dulcie did wake up, but she didn't fuss at all. She just looked around at everyone, including all the crabby old ladies, and smiled. Once again I wait for the clincher, but that's all there is to that story.

It's Friday, and my ax is poised to chop Lily's stories out of the sermon in favor of the other stories, which fit cleanly into the columns I've allotted for naming grace. However, Lily's stories have been working on me all week. I see Arvo and Lily grinding up to church, short-legged Lily clambering down from the dump truck in her Sunday-go-to-meeting clothes. The rest of the flock watches from Saturday-washed sedans as Arvo rumbles away in a cloud of diesel exhaust. I am beginning to see how Arvo may have brought Lily closer to Jesus, and I wonder how Jesus himself might have preached this scene. Maybe he'd present it just as Lily told it, letting the people remember themselves as they watched Lily clamber down and Arvo drive away. Maybe Jesus would let them draw their own conclusions.

Just so, I have come to feel the weight of Dulcie's body, the fine gold of her hair, the heat of the church on a lazy July day, the dread of the mother, the censorious oppression of the women around her, and Dulcie's unexpected awakening smiles. Still, I can't connect this story with my experience of closeness to Jesus. I finally decide that this is Lily's story, her witness to her community. I resist the temptation to fabricate some neat ending, but I wonder what the congregation will make of it.

As it turned out, the stories of other faith mentors brought smiles of recognition, remembrance, and even some tears. Courtney had never been able to tell Bonnie that the bedtime prayers at her daughter's sleep overs had brought Courtney closer to Jesus. Bonnie's eyes began to glisten as she heard herself presented as a teacher of prayer in her community, as she began to see herself, and the congregation began to see her, in a new light.

Then I told Lily's stories. They, too, elicited some smiles. And Lily herself must have appreciated the irony. Years have passed, and Dulcie is now not only a mother, but also a grandmother, and since Arvo's passing a decade ago, Lily sits with other widows where the crabby old ladies once sat. I felt the stillness and watched the absolute focus of those I was sure could also feel that child on their laps. The assembled community was squinting together, trying to see Jesus come down the opening road. I felt it, but I still didn't see it. But sometime later, my friend Sherri remarked, "You told Lily about Samuel and Eli. Dulcie's story is an awakening story."

If that is so, we are all waking up to find ourselves already in the story we love. Mothers and fathers notice their children listening, looking up from their coloring books or their little bags of Froot Loops when they hear mention of a familiar name, or the Pine Cone Café, or a bulldozer in a story about Jesus. Now, even four-year-olds know this story is for them.

I think that I have stumbled on to something revolutionary. I believe that I am as hip as Baz Luhrmann whose film, *William Shakespeare's Romeo & Juliet*, features tattoos and Hawaiian shirts, as well as the dialogue from the classic text. If only I had two hours, a million-dollar budget, and Leonardo DiCaprio and Clare Danes, my casino sermon, for instance, would look like this film! But it turns out this is an old idea. In 1652 George Herbert wrote about the parson preaching: "He procureth attention by all possible art: . . . with particularizing of his speech now to the younger sort, then to the elder, now to the poor, and now to the rich—'this is for you, and this is for you'; for particulars ever touch, and awake, more than generals."[19]

THE LINK

What happens when we make these connections, creating sparks across the gaps—when Shakespearean dialogue and the classic text of *Romeo and Juliet* are linked with the world of tattoos, Hawaiian shirts, and rock 'n' roll? This shocking collision of a world we recognize and a world we assumed we'd never understand without a hopeless array of lexicons and Cliffs Notes, might jolt us into the realization that this old story is, in fact, for us.

What happens when we join our marketplace words for the bread we spread with peanut butter, the bread for which a child in India cries out for, the crumbs the Canaanite woman begs for her daughter, the boy's lunch bread that Jesus lifts and shares on a hillside, the bread on the altar, and the Bread of Life? Will Jesus meet us in this multiverse where boundaries become thin and worlds collide, creating new perceptions of reality in which God is revealed as the center of all life, for us?

Naming grace is really *naming* grace, awakening us to new life by linking the ordinary particularities of real lives in a familiar world with the expansive possibilities of the holy and the realm of God in the story we long to break into. When we link words like "user," "taker," "clueless," "slimebucket" to the Parable of the Unforgiving Servant, we prepare to discover that this story is about people we know, about us. When "the One" or "the Messiah" suddenly shows up in a Toivo and Eino joke, we know we're not in Kansas (or at least not simply in Upper Michigan) anymore. These words, sticking out in the story and changing its *text*-ure, function as signposts, pointing from one world to another. This is the work of metaphor, linking two distinct worlds of meaning, often using a more familiar source to help us apprehend a new or less familiar reality. Howard Nemerov, former poet laureate of the United States, is remembered to have commented that in Greece, *metaphores* is a common word for "moving van."[20] We bundle up our household treasures, ferry them to new surroundings, and discover something different about both the old and the new.

But a local joke here and there, with a casino or even a bulldozer thrown in, will not suffice for the "new thing" that householders bring out of the storehouse. You can't just dress a sermon up in marketplace garb and give it nowhere to go out in the world. Aim for the chopping block. Not for the wood. In Baz Luhrmann's version of *Romeo and Juliet*, the tattoos, leather jackets, and earrings are not mere spectacle, not trivializing dead ends: Luhrmann's "point is not to distract you from the words . . . but to lead you to them."[21] And the words lead us out the doors of the past into a story that is pointed for us today—the world our children inherit, violence in families and on the streets, the love of power and the power of love, the cost of long-standing enmity, and the role of the Church in reconciling lives and communities.

Jesus walks into the Temple at Jerusalem, but it bears a great resemblance to one of our local gambling casinos. There are snowmobiles and pickup trucks on the "altar." When the Temple tax is being paid out in casino chips, and Jesus asks whose inscription they bear, we know that this story about who rules and who saves is as much for us today as it was for people 2,000 years ago. We know that we are about to hear a Word that will cleave, that will expose and lay open the deeply held concerns we have for our community, the people and the places that affect us deeply. We can no longer distinguish between us and them; we can no longer separate the lives we lead inside the church building from the lives we lead outside it. Worlds are colliding. God is breaking through the barriers of space, time, print on page with a Word, for us.

When our names (or the names of people we know) literally put a name to grace, when Jack and Ester and Gretchen and Stanley are linked to Toivo and Eino and Philip, Nathaniel, and Jesus—we are connected to our local traditions, to the faith tradition, and to one another in new ways. In the same way we are surprised to find treasure in a field, the pearl worth everything, and fish of all kinds in one net, the familiar story of God's love becomes new when we find ourselves in God's household in the midst of our daily lives. When asked what she found recognizable in the sermon from the marketplace, one woman commented: "Well, *I* was mentioned in the sermon; it was about *me* being in the marketplace!" When asked whether the marketplace setting made the Bible story more real and understandable to her Stacy answered, "Well, I was *there*!" as if I had unexpectedly asked a dumb question.

Being there, on the interface between gospel and world, and then *being shown as being there*, makes the sermon world, the textual world, and the marketplace world transparent to one another. This transparency allows all these worlds to be shown for what they are: the arena for God's activity, the lively space into which the rule of God may be breaking—a world we may inhabit. Naming grace can make us "insiders" to the gospel, can link two worlds we weren't certain could be linked, and can cause an impact that breaks us right into the world of its life-giving story.

Bruce, our congregational president, township supervisor, and an area logger, awakened me to the ways naming grace can link us to one another as faith companions and guides. He was in the sacristy counting the offering when I mumbled something to my husband about speeding and polishing up my delivery for the next service. Bruce perked up. "What's delivery?" asked this man, who sets his coffee cup on the stained-glass windowsill when he comes to worship. And takes a sip, I swear, just to let me know when I'm putting him to sleep. "Oh," he responded, as I explained that it meant my performance, my pace and articulation. "Well, who the hell cares about that? Just give me some everyday people I can connect with, and I'll listen all day. That's what I care about."

Too often our sermons are like my husband's 8 mm movies from a trip to the Apostle Islands—frame after frame of lonely gulls and barren seascape. "Where are the people?" his family teases, gently adding that "that's what we care about." People's lives, writes F. Dean Lueking, ". . . speak to us. Their experiences move and bless us. This is the sense of invitation that the marvelous mercy of God extends. Christ's grace reaches others through those whose very lives are an invitation to taste and see that the Lord is good."[22]

"Hearers discover in such preaching," states James Nieman, "the many different roles of discipleship open to them and which of these they are able, through Christ, to adopt." In sermons preached from the marketplace, hearers-turned-proclaimers also discover Christian friends with whom they can link up, real people to whom they can apprentice themselves for discipleship. These are people who, preaching in our kitchens, driving our dump trucks and bulldozers, tucking our kids in with prayer on overnights ". . . declare through . . . ordinary lives that the faith is doable and the gospel can make a difference in the world, not simply in the church."[23] Bill Diehl, a layperson and former sales manager for Bethlehem Steel, observes that "pastors are not always the appropriate people to consult when a Christian is trying to relate faith to daily life. Pastors are not competent to provide counsel in all types of problems, nor should they be expected to do so. So where do we go with the more technical problems? We go to the church, the community of believers."[24] The pastor's "work of God," alone with the ax in that castle on Fridays, may very well be in aiming to provide this linkage of those whose work of God is in the world *through* the sermon, out the doors, so that the congregation transforms society.

This contemporary hagiography of real people not only awakens us to the struggles and the resources we can share with one another, but it also serves to point us toward the lives of the faithful in the tradition. Nieman notes that "ancient hagiographies and martyrologies presented the lives of saints and martyrs as ones to be followed, not because they were people who were 'bigger-than-life' but precisely because they were ordinary folks whom God had made extraordinary."[25] When we link ourselves to this tradition through here-and-now saints, the faithful who have gone before us become newly available as mentors as well. In the epistle lesson for the celebration of the Confession of Peter, Peter and John (ordinary men, only one of whom, we note, ever seems to do or say anything extraordinary) are on trial for the healing of the man at the Temple gates. In my sermon for this day, I linked Saint Peter's and Saint John's work of God with Lois's, Jane's, and Sandy's work in raising the "invisible" among us to full participation in the life of the community. Lois integrates low-functioning adults into everyday activities; Sandy educates people with diabetes, helping them live more fully despite the disease; and Jane offers Bible study at a substance-abuse rehabilitation center. Through the gift of community we can become, like John, silent partners in their everyday acts of healing. "Members of Trinity Lutheran Church show how what seem little acts are opportunities for God to act," Doris suggests. But through them, Peter and John have also become our mentors: "Seeing and understanding Peter and John in relation to our own community and peers made this story so much more interesting and understandable and made me much more aware."

Offering apprenticeships in healings at the Temple gates makes sense for those whose preaching is done not in pulpits but in those other sacred spaces of our lives and communities where we find ourselves without last Sunday's manuscript to whip out of our shirt pockets. Preaching is done every day, when we speak up at a board meeting, respond to the insistent pressure of a peer to shoplift, offer condolences as we pass through the line at a wake. Preaching is done in the spaces between the interruptions of the phone, the wail of the baby, or the whaling of children upon one another. Studied masterpieces of convoluted reasoning will not be fitting forms for a word that can raise the dead, break through our insensibilities, and sound like good news when we are harassed and helpless. Our masterpieces will not be there to serve us when at any moment we may be called to squint into the viewfinder with others to see the road on which Jesus comes to us, when it comes down to reflex. "Be careful how you live," advises Sarah, a member of my evangelism committee. "Your life may be the only Bible your neighbor will ever read."

THE BARD

The Sunday morning preacher who has stood sans backpack in the marketplace comes to Friday morning with a keen understanding that it is only what people are able to remember that will be available for these encounters where the sermon has to live. Our Friday work of God which we approach as "trained scribes," certainly calls for craft. But if the sermon offered on Sunday *appears* to be crafted and bears no resemblance to the patterns, rhythms, and words we use every day outside the church doors, we are sending another kind of signal: that the language of the faith is "speech for hire." This is the kind of specialized knowledge and vocabulary that your plumber uses, or your mechanic, or lawyer. This is knowledge for which the rest of us can imagine no real use at the kitchen table or Pine Cone Café.[26] Diehl reminds us that "words like salvation, creation, redemption, sanctification must be given meaning in the language of the workplace, otherwise, lay people cannot connect their Sunday worship with their weekday world."[27]

As we aim for the chopping block, cleaving worlds along the grain of our lives, hoping to meet Jesus on the road, what songs will our axes be singing? "If the message we sing is ever to leave the confines of the church," Nieman suggests, "it must be borne through the lives and voices of those who hear it, who may sing it quite differently than we would, but in ways perhaps more appropriate to the world than we might ever imagine."[28] We might take some singing lessons from the bards whose epic poems were sung in the marketplace. The bards stitched their songs together from scraps of familiar patterns and themes, often beginning in the thick of the action. Their songs revolved around familiar refrains and were drawn from the oft-told story that became new in the "interaction between the singer, the singer's current audience, and the singer's memories of songs sung."[29]

Perhaps scribes like Matthew were in the line of such bards, stitching together parables "in the manner of Jesus" or "in the manner of Mark," introducing a variation on the theme, making their particulars "for" the current audience. Matthew portrays Jesus as such a bard, going to the storehouse of commonly held metaphors and stories that, over time, had built up connections that serve as signposts between real and symbolic worlds.[30] Matthew knows Jesus' and every bard's secret: the new song is not radically different from the old songs. It is not even innovative. It is an old, cherished story in lively interface with our stories that becomes new for us.

The songs we sing as scribes who have been trained for the rule of God will be crafted from the gatherings around our table, from discussions of the ins and outs of the texts with the best scholars our commentaries can afford, and from the peopled landscape of the marketplace. Because we are paid for their composition, these songs may well be speech for hire. But when we conceive these songs in the manner of the bard, as songs that are to be sung in the market square, we may stitch together even a text-based consciousness into a kind of epic of God's love for the world, with memorable choruses in which everyone might join.

☙❧

It is the Friday after bulldozing with Larry, and I can already feel the rumble of the pickup trucks, maybe even Arvo's dump truck, heading for our appointed Sunday's picnic in the wilderness. I take aim to preach Jesus, but first I answer the phone. It's Larry, calling with the news about Karen's and Tom's baby. It's a girl. Emily. "Great," I tell him, taking down the particulars to share in church. "Say, Larry? I'm just getting down to writing the sermon, and it looks like the way it's going, I may just want to talk about our day together. Would that be OK?" "Sure, pastor. However I can help," says Larry. "But listen. It's my birthday this weekend, and I'm heading up to camp right now. We've got a bunch of people coming, so I'm not sure I'll be there in church. Hope it goes well for you though." I mentally calculate that half the congregation will be parking their pickups at Larry's camp this Sunday. "Hey, happy birthday, Larry! And thanks for the news about the baby."

NOTES

1. Ebeling, *Word and Faith*, 329–31. Ebeling describes the sermon as the "execution" of the text, where the sermon performs not the text itself, but its *aims*, an understanding not *of* language, but *through* language, that opens new possibilities for the here-and-now hearer.

2. Byatt, *Possession*, 379.

3. *Ibid.*

4. Rose, *Sharing the Word*, 97. Rose summarizes Smith, *Weaving the Sermon*, 47, 52.

5. *Ibid.* Much of Rose's work in collaborative preaching aims at eradicating this gap.

6. *Ibid.* 136, n. 6. Rose opens this possibility as she considers how Chopp construes "gaps" as lively space where God breaks into the world, where new things are given room to come into being.

7. Schreiter, *Construing Local Theologies*, 16–20. Schreiter speaks from his perspective as a missiologist on the gifts of the insider and outsider to the community. Not every Christian needs to have the grasp of the tradition expected of the professional theologian, but his concern is that the gap not grow in a way that concentrates information as "power over."

8. Bornkamm, *Luther in Mid-Career*, 49–50. "It was from Luther's Bible that the German people learned to speak the language they were to have in common."

9. Schreiter, 39–49. Schreiter borrows the phrase, "listening heart" from Raymond Facelina, "Une theologie en situation," *Revue des Sciences Religieuses* 48, (1974), 320.

10. Tisdale, *Preaching as Local Theology and Folk Art*, 49–55. Tisdale has a helpful section on the outsider and insider roles preachers can play as local theologians.

11. Schreiter, 58–59. The outsider perspective can assist the culture in its transition point to a new identity. The outsider serves the inside culture by telling insiders what is happening to them and providing links to a larger reality.

12. Tisdale, 56–90. Tisdale offers insight into discerning congregational ethos: when that ethos is to be honored and affirmed and when it may be fruitfully stretched and challenged.

13. Ptomey, "A Cry in the Night," 33. "We live with fractured relationships, troubled marriages, problems with our children, addiction, grief, unreconciled differences with people we deeply care about. But, for whatever reasons, our pain does not find an avenue for public expression."

14. Wilson-Kastner, *Imagery for Preaching*, 57–58, and Wilson, *The Practice of Preaching*, 251. Wilson writes, "Name and denounce evil, do not paint it in detail, for it is not evil that we preach, but God's condemnation of it and victory over it in Jesus Christ."

15. Hilkert, *Naming Grace*, 110. "For some in the community, pain and abuse continue to isolate precisely because they remain invisible and unspoken." For resources about giving voice to the silenced, the unspeakable, and to that which seem beyond language, see Hilkert, chap. 7; Smith, *Preaching as Weeping, Confession, and Resistence*; Edgerton, *The Passion of Interpretation*, chap. 5; Allen, *Preaching the Topical Sermon*, chap. 5; and Trible, *Texts of Terror*, 2.

16. Schreiter, 59.

17. Hilkert, 186–87.

18. Schreiter, 16–18.

19. Herbert, *The Parson Preaching*, found in Lischer, *Theories of Preaching*, 52.

20. Nemerov, *Reflexions on Poetry and Poetics*, 90. Metaphor is associated with the verb *bear*, "arousing the . . . idea of being born, of how thoughts, like children, come out of the nowhere into the here . . ." This is also the power of revelatory poesis to which Ricoeur refers: "So too the new being projected by the biblical text opens its way across the world of everyday experience. . . .The power to project this new world is the power of breaking through, and of opening." Ricoeur, *Toward a Hermeneutic of the Idea of Revelation*, 102.

21. Travers, "Just Two Kids in Love," 123–24.

22. Lueking, *Preaching: The Art of Connecting God and People*, 21, 27.

23. Nieman, *Preaching That Drives People from Church*, 113, 115.

24. Diehl, *The Monday Connection*, 48.

25. Nieman, 115.

26. Ong, *Orality and Literacy*, 94.

27. Diehl, 10. Deihl reflects on Droel and Pierce, *Confident and Competent*, 42.

28. Nieman, 112.

29. Ong, 59, 146.

30. Boring, "Matthew Introduction and Commentary," 314

All of Them Are Alive

"O that my words were . . . engraved on a rock forever!" (Job 19:23–27a)

Jesus speaks about the resurrection.(Luke 20:27–38)

Peggy's Version

Peggy and I went looking for signs of life at the cemetery this week.

"We're not too imaginative in Amasa," Peggy said, as we took Cemetery Road over Cemetery Creek past Cemetery Lake to Hematite Township Cemetery. "Do you want to visit the old cemetery, the old new cemetery, or the *new* new cemetery?" she asked.

The old cemetery was overgrown and scary when Peggy was growing up. On one of their first dates, Phil took her on a path into the woods to see the graves of the Hansen babies, all by themselves in a little grove. Baby Ruth's old cedar marker is still back there, leaning against a tree. Alongside it is a beautiful statue of Mary standing in the stars and clouds. Her feet are crushing the head of the serpent through whose temptation death is said to have first come into the world.

It's hard to escape the connection between sin and death when you make a cemetery walk. Over in the old new cemetery, passing Donny Maki's grave, Peggy remembers the first time she was conscious of sin. It was the day that she stole a big sucker out of Donny's playhouse. This was closely followed by her first lie, when her mom asked her where she got such a sucker, and Peggy said, "Oh, Mrs. Maki gave it to me!" We've come here to know the sting of death that is sin.

We also come to find out who we are, in the company of those who have gone before us. Peggy's Grandpa Leanna's stone is dated 1957, just two days before Peggy's birthday. She never knew her grandfather, but her mother tells her the story every time they visit this grave. Peggy knows she had been waited for. Grandpa Leanna had been waiting just for her to be born, to see "what" she was. Nancy went into labor with Peggy the morning of the funeral. She didn't tell any of the women in the house, who were baking biscuit for the lunch. She didn't want to go to the hospital until it was out of the oven and she could have a bite. So the way I figure it, Peg never had a chance against her craving for Little Debbies snacks!

Even though Peggy never even knew her grandpa in this life, she still has a special relationship with him. He is alive to her in telling this story of his life and death that has such a close connection with her own birth.

Our relationships to our loved ones continue to grow and change and heal, even after death. At the women's fall retreat at Fortune Lake this year, a number of women went to see Pastor Cy's grave for the first time. "I need to see him, talk to him, let him know what's happened with me," one told me. "Time to forgive our last fight," a woman decided. "Time to realize he's finally well and whole," still another said.

Our relationships with those we love are never over. Death can't end them. One grave stone spells out, "Son, we love you forever." Another: "O love that would not let me go." I don't know whether this one is talking about God's love or our love that doesn't let go in death, but maybe there is not much difference. For God and for the children of the resurrection, love is stronger than death; love and life go on.

We see it everywhere we lay loved ones to rest. John Tusa's ashes were scattered at the Triangle Ranch. On the way in, we passed outbuildings caving in, wanting to go back to the earth. But up on the hill, there were tons of wild strawberries. They stained our fingers with the goodness of life before we let him go. This fall, Brenda took Tynne out to the cemetery so that before snow flies they could plant tulips in the promise of spring to come.

Families sometimes plant a little square around their stones, to say, Nothing will separate us, we'll be together forever. Most of those stones tell who we are to one another. Son, Mother, Father, Stepmother.

Some say "infant." It's amazing how many children were taken by illnesses penicillin can cure now. These babies were carefully named, their brief days exactly numbered. Their graves look wept over, cherished. One little life, that lasted only a few days, already many decades ago, is still cared for tenderly. The grave is nestled under a tree, with turtles and a little bunny figurine placed there to keep it company. In the cemetery, we see more plainly than almost anywhere else that life matters.

"O that the story of my struggle with God and life would be written down and preserved for posterity," cries Job. "Not on perishable paper! Chisel my life and its story on rock to last forever," he demands. "Engrave into copper my faithfulness to God, my battle with failing health, the injustice of my losses, my love for my children, so that such a monument will stand as a lasting witness against the ravages of time."

We want such monuments. Lasting records of our love, our life, our struggles. Our veterans have bronze memorials that tell their rank and their war and their place of service. The stones that date back to the Great Depression days may be nothing more than poured concrete. The names may be laboriously inscribed, tiny dots pounded onto thin strips of tin, letter by letter. Some of the new stones are beautiful. Vic Kivimaki's stone sings a song of love for his camp on the Net River. Other's have deer on them, or skidders, or Bibles. Peggy wants hers wallpapered—and changed every year!

Some stones are carved with wedding rings or hearts. Some have the names of still-living husbands or wives engraved on them, even when they've gone on to marry again, to say love never ends. Many of your names are already on stones waiting only for the date when you are reunited with loved ones. You know already where you will one day rest. Doris says that one day she was surprised by a birthday card from a fifth-grade math student. When Doris asked the girl how she had known her birthday, the student told her that she'd seen it on Doris's gravestone! Maybe it is *life* that is marked on our graves.

These engraved monuments last longer than paper or cedar posts, but they won't last forever. Joe Nash at the funeral home tells me that even bronze gets pounded down and worn by rain and snow. Some stones are already overgrown, covered by moss and mildew. Some are hardly readable—soft Georgia granite doesn't stand up to our Northern weather.

One of my favorite stones has faded so that I can barely make out the design. It's a double gate, swinging out into what looks like a beautiful future, telling the story of the psalm that Fred and I read as a funeral procession comes to the grave: "Open for me the gates of righteousness; I will enter them; I will offer thanks to the Lord."(Psalm 118:19)

This is on a Peltonen stone: Eino Ketola's grandparents on his mother's side, just behind Sanna and John, his dad's folks. Next to them is their son Alexander, who died in a mining accident with three others when a cage cable broke. His wife, Lydia, was pregnant, and the baby was stillborn that day. Baby Toivo's grave is next to Alexander's; they share the same date. Lydia was left with three girls and three other boys to support. She took in washing, made hay, and wallpapered. One of these sons was Waino Ketola, who married Ines, a school teacher. They settled in Stambaugh, and they went to our sister church there. Waino fought in both theaters during the Second World War, and he came home hurt the second time. Despite their struggles, they had a good life. Their son Warren worked for 3M and had something to do with inventing the glue for Post-it notes. Ines and Waino were buried in the Stambaugh cemetery.

Even our Stambaugh and Amasa cemeteries are connected. By love. By struggles. By faith. In the stories of the lives of the faithful of both our congregations, those we thought were dead are alive to us and in us. Because they are available to us as we remember them, we are strengthened for our own losses and lives to continue our course on earth in confidence.

We need faith and confidence because there is so much that tests the promises of God. This includes the pain and power of tragedy, death, and loss. We come to the cemetery looking for some kind of guarantee. Are our loved ones in heaven? Will we join them there? How will we know them? What really happens to us when we die?

That was one field trip I couldn't take for you. I can go only as far as the cemetery and the stones. The same as you. And there I see expressed our faith and our belief that life matters and love never dies.

But there *is* someone who has been there and back: Jesus, the faithful witness to God's plan. Jesus is to be raised himself in just a few days when he tells us in today's Gospel that life matters. He proclaims that love never dies, but that our life in God after death won't be a continuation of life on earth. It will be something different.

Peggy figures we can't understand it now, but it's got to be a great surprise. It will be something we couldn't guess, but something that will be so familiar and obvious when we get to it. God wouldn't give us these close relationships, these people with whom we can't wait to be reunited, she says, and not do something with that.

Brian, at the funeral home, thinks maybe this is what we are being prepared for in our rituals of grief. When our loved ones die and we remember them, when we tell their stories, we begin to be close to them. We come to know them in a new way—more like the way we will know them in heaven.

Maybe our eternal life together resembles the way our Stambaugh and Amasa cemeteries are connected through Alexander Ketola and Waino Ketola, only bigger. Eternal life will be like a family reunion—a big family-wedding celebration—only *everyone* will be like family. We will be united across all the gulfs that separate us. All of God's children will know the closeness of that love that never dies.

Our monuments will weather and one day return to the earth. Even our memories will fade. But to my friend Joe Sittler, whose churchyard resting place I visited this summer, belonging by baptism to this God of the living meant this: "In the mind of God, we shall never not have been. That's enough."

Jesus proclaims this mystery of faith for us in announcing that our God is a God not of the dead but of the living. To this powerful God, all of them are alive. In Jesus, amidst all the uncertainties that life and death can throw at us, we know this one true thing: Our life is in God, and God does not die. Amen.

Chapter 4

The Sermon as Crafted: Making It Memorable

All the parts of preaching can be taught. . . . What is hard to teach is how to put them all together, so that what is true is also beautiful and evocative and alive.

—Barbara Brown Taylor, *The Preaching Life*

[Jesus says] Lift up the stone and you will find me there. Split a piece of wood and you will find me there.

—Greek Thomas 30:3–4

But Jesus said to them, "You do not know what you're asking. Are you able to drink the cup that I drink, or be baptized with the baptism that I am baptized with?" They replied, "We are able." [Jesus said to them] "Whoever wishes to be great among you must be your servant, and whoever wishes to be first among you must be the slave of all. For the Son of Man came not to be served but to serve, and to give his life a ransom for many."

—Mark 10:38–45

So where do I begin? How do I put all the parts together in a way that will make them memorable in the places in which they have to live? I wonder whether all my Saturday nights as an ax-wielding bard are destined to be hellish, desperately producing mounds of chips, hacking a way through dense forest to some sort of sermon—never mind cleaving worlds.

Not every sermon has to be a story, but stories help organize a lot of details we want to remember. Storytellers of yore had to remember the entire history, wisdom, craft, and survival system of the community, and they encoded all this information in their poems.[1] Some stories, especially stories in which we play a part or long to break into, we may hear once and remember forever. George Herbert knew that back in 1652: "Sometimes he tells them the sayings of others, according as his text invites him: for these also men heed, and remember better than exhortations; which, though earnest, yet often die with the sermon; . . . but stories and sayings they will well remember."[2]

Not every sermon has to be a story, but every sermon has one. This chapter is a tale of two sermons.

UP TO OUR NECKS . . .
RAY WESTPHAL: PRESIDENT AND SERVANT

It is another Friday, and once again I feel as if I am up to my neck in it. "For the Son of Man came not to be served but to serve, and to give his life a ransom for many." Mark 10:45 is a difficult song, and it is not easy to get others to sing it with you. But there is plenty of action—the backstory of the Transfiguration and Jesus' announcement of the Passion, incongruous dreams of glory for James and John, the all-too-realistic bickering among the disciples, Jesus' enigmatic sayings about drinking the cup.

Things happen in the story of the marketplace too. At Ray's Golden K meeting, I witness his servant leadership of headstrong disciples. And I find Vanessa in the kitchen at her friend's benefit, up to her neck in dirty dishes. Art had set me up with Tullio, whose story about life as a raw recruit and prisoner of war in World War II he already finds compelling, and there is plenty more. Gary tells me that since our Bible study he's been thinking about what military service meant in his family. Paul B. brings me his three favorite books, whose stories of service and sacrifice express a meaning he is also able to sing for himself when he brings them to me and we talk over coffee.

I am overwhelmed by this embarrassment of riches, a net filled with fish of every kind, and I am swimming in it. I suspend panic. I pour myself a cup of coffee. I sit on my castle floor with an orchestral-score-size piece of paper. I make three columns and leave the middle column blank. In the first column I write:

What are the simple, clean forms of the tale *that must be there*?

James & John come forward wanting to sit in glory. They *step up* to discipleship, but desire to place themselves *ahead* of the crowd.

Jesus: You don't know what you're asking. Are you able to drink the cup?" (Old Testament symbol for intense experiences, both good and painful).[3] Can you be with me "up to your necks"? (Old Testament vernacular related to baptism.)[4]

James and John: "We are able!"

Jesus (sighing): "You will do this. You will get into the strong stuff, you will be in up to your necks. But glory? Position? Who knows?" Not a statement about how life *should be* lived, but an acknowledgment of *how* life is.

The other disciples get angry.

Jesus: "You know how you hate it when others look down on you. (*kata* means both "over people" or "looking down, being higher up." Contrast between way of the world with rank and privilege, and the way of Jesus' followers. In Jesus' body there is no rank like this.)[5]

"For us, it will be as equals. I have come to serve, not to be served, and give my life to free people (from what?)"

In the column on the other side of the page, I write:

What made this old story seem *new, first seen in the marketplace*?

GROUP: Examples of "blowhard politicians," "people looking out for number one."

VANESSA: Image of volunteerism was glorious, exciting. The reality was that it turns out to be hard work! But, there is joy, and it pulls people together. Nobody could have told her this.

TULLIO: Love of country. Guys are *gung ho* in basic training. Nobody can tell you what it's really like. Then you get there. Raw survival. Captured, imprisoned. Red Cross boxes as sustenance. Sometimes feels badly about his service—never got to do what he was *supposed* to do because he got caught. *Couldn't escape.*

VANESSA and STACY: Band at football games. Freezing fingers on sax; and service while the team gets the glory. Youth experience of glory and service.

GARY: Dad. Love kept him going; the vision of the Virgin of Guadelupe who *came to live* with the people of Mexico and *share their humble life*. Mom lost a finger in munitions plant. Mom's and Dad's service *equal*, and *equal* to his own, even if he never got to serve in country.

RAY: Mountaintop presidential installation. Next day, reality hits. Calls for volunteers: silence. They change subject to what *they* want to do. Finally, "I'll be there. Who's coming with me?" Servant leadership. I see that text is not about a willingness to die but about being willing to lead without flaunting authority.[6]

PAUL B.: Basic training changes from someone who wants to be served (American "civilian" culture) to someone who serves. When you're "up to your necks in it," you see life differently. Love makes it possible.

I take another sip of coffee. I squint hard and aim to split the two stories open, down the center column, along the grain of our lives, writing:

What is God doing here that reveals God as the center of every life?

> ☞ Going first, inviting us to follow

> ☞ Standing behind Jesus: our ministry as servant/leaders

- Making us *able* to drink of the cup, the powerful stuff of life, both pleasurable and painful, letting us experience it for ourselves

- Offering up Jesus to free and ransom us from our underlying issues of inadequacy and insufficiency

- Making service possible through love: If James and John finally are able, it is because of Jesus' love for them, their love for Jesus, and their love for those whom Jesus came to ransom

- Reversing our values by determining what glory is, making all our service equal and valid

- Transforming us who are up to our necks through baptism into Jesus' death and resurrection

Now I draw lines from one column to another, aiming toward Jesus, aiming out the doors into the marketplace where this song would have to be remembered in order to be sung. I trace the voices that connect. I am looking for the familiar refrains, the lively currency of marketplace exchange, places where worlds collide unexpectedly. I eye them as a merchant sorts through pearls. I find *in it up to our necks*. I find *the cup*.

I find my group member Paul who was transformed by basic training—from an individual who wants to be served to a person whose life is on the line and is in it up to his neck.

Transformed, like James and John, he sees life as being bound to others in a love that makes service and sacrifice possible, even glorious. I find Gary and Tullio, struggling with our community's underlying concern, sometimes masked by: "Why should we care?" But really deep down, they wonder, "How do we measure up? Are we able?" I find Vanessa mirroring Tullio's memories of the raw recruits, for whom basic training is no substitute for real experience. And I find Jesus, who takes a leaf from Ray and goes first, inviting others to follow him into service.

Where do I begin the song, composing it from these treasures, new and old? I decide to begin with Ray. Of course, it's Ray. The Ray we all know as the one who'll come out in the middle of the night to fix a broken furnace. But it's also Ray, president of the Golden Ks, who stands as representative of all the leaders who are forever trying to muster the volunteer troops. "Patient Ray" is not an epic, larger-than-life figure like Homer's "clever Odysseus" perhaps, but he is an ordinary one who will make worlds collide by apprenticing us for discipleship: Clearly, Jesus and Ray are apprenticed to one another.

I give the president of the Golden Ks a call. "Ray," I say, "is it OK if I use your story about getting volunteers for the old-time dance in my sermon this week? Don't worry. You'll look pretty good up there!"

This is how this story starts:

> *Just the night before, Ray Westphal had been installed as president of the Golden Ks. I wasn't there, but I know it was preceded by dinner at Alice's. The next morning, though, I was at the Iron River Senior Citizens' Center, when Ray was wishing that he had a gavel to bring down to call those Golden Ks to order.*

Ray's story begins with the mountaintop installation dinner at Alice's Supper Club (special-occasion dining) that contrasts with the morning-after meeting of the Golden Ks at the Senior Citizens' Center (a much humbler, "everyday" place to eat). These places are full of memories of songs sung—songs that set the scene for us. Now we may be adding new associations—layering meanings and memories—as we begin to remember Alice's and the Senior Center as places where the gospel story may be breaking in.

> *Behind him, a set of wooden letters spelled out P-R-E-S-I-D-E-N-T. Just a few hours earlier, he'd received that gift amidst applause and encouragement. Now, Ray was in it up to his neck . . . I'm not sure exactly what Ray was thinking at this point, but I wondered whether he had known that it was going to be like this when he had stood up there at Alice's and said, "I will." "I am able" to serve as president of the Golden Ks.*

Bardlike, I compose this whole song around the refrain "in it up to his neck." It is a contemporary colloquialism but also an old treasure, rich in scriptural vernacular for baptism.[7] Memorable for the bard (but also memorable and repeatable for everyone out in the market square), catchphrases, proverbs, and even clichés are woven into the song. This lively currency of marketplace exchange is repeated throughout the epic so that we can remember it, each time bringing past associations and adding something new.[8]

The bard would also use "communal fixed formulas"[9] (what we might call "liturgies") that everyone knows and that are memorable and associative. "I will. I am able" is a liturgy of installation or a renewal of baptismal promises that is also a feature of the gospel story, making the worlds of secular volunteerism, baptismal covenant, and gospel story transparent to one another.

> *The Jesus of our story today would have been able to sympathize with Ray. Not too much earlier than the events in today's gospel lesson, he had stood on a mountaintop with Peter and James and John. God's voice had showered approval over Jesus, naming him God's beloved one, and Moses and Elijah stood to Jesus' right and left in the power and the glory.*

Ray's story, as it unfolds in the marketplace, cuts the pattern for this gospel song just a little wide of the pericope, back to the story of Transfiguration. Peter and James and John, Moses and Elijah, right and left, the power and the glory are rhythmic formulas that help us remember.

Now I stitch this old story in as a variation on a theme of volunteerism as experienced in the marketplace. We know what is going to happen to Ray, because we know the Golden Ks. They are like us: an unruly, sometimes difficult-to-motivate bunch! Nevertheless, we like to hear this story. We're insiders anticipating and relishing the punch lines. And we also know how this gospel story will turn out: the disciples are like us. Anticipating how the story turns out, we become insiders, disciples, who can name the grace in this song, anywhere.

> *James and John are like gung ho recruits who are done with basic training and eager to get into the glory of battle. They can't possibly know what they are getting into, and what it will be like*

when the shells explode: What it will be like when they drink of
the cup of intensity, the strong stuff of life; when they find them-
selves in it, up to their necks. . . . And glory is not there for all.
Maybe for some. But if it is there for you, the chances are you
will have suffered on the way to it. There's no substitute for expe-
rience, thinks Jesus, looking into their future. If you continue to
follow me, you will *get into the strong stuff. You* will *be in up to*
your necks. You won't be able to escape it. . . .

I hadn't planned on retelling the biblical story, but in my orchestral
score my friends the veterans kept making connections across the
lines to the phrasing of this old story and to the original connections
my group had made in sending me to them in the first place. I stitch
in Paul B.'s own words and phrases about military service. These
words may be memorable back in the marketplace because they
sound like something we'd say in conversation.

The bard would keep things interesting for both himself and the
hearer, not by producing new thoughts in terms of original ideas—
because ideas had been hard-won and painstakingly gathered in
memory—but by offering variations on well-known themes.[10]

Our refrains circle in theme and variation throughout this story, too:
drinking the cup; up to our necks in it; Jesus, pointing out that in fact
we *will*. We will, not because we should, or because we will to, but
just because life is that way. Although we've been led to believe that
we know what is coming in these stories, seeing the gospel through
Paul B.'s story of recruit training shows that serving, discipleship,
glory, and rewards will be somewhat different from what we have
imagined. Old story, new insight. We discover that all those church
words have real meaning in real lives, and God is revealed at the center of it all.

Glory may be bravery on the front lines. Or it may be the army
nurse working seventeen hour days, or a woman stateside who
lost a finger working in a munitions factory when the men went
to war. The services of a prisoner of war or of a volunteer who
packed a Red Cross box are of the same value here, Jesus says.
You will all be up to your necks in it . . . every time we offer our-

selves to liberate, to set free another, it carries the same reward. For, Jesus said, the Son of Man came not to be served, but to serve, and to give his life a ransom for many . . .

Grace isn't named here, in the midst of struggle. But it could be. Each of these people has a name, and I wonder whether to use them. I decide that a litany of names would be cumbersome and distracting. Aim for the chopping block, not the wood, I remind myself. And life's situation of struggle and bravery of all sorts are what I want people to get to. In the marketplace, we often find ourselves in conflict or problem-solving situations. We hope this story, this sermon, our faith, those to whom we are apprenticed in discipleship, will be able to give us meaning and guidance for those situations.[11]

I don't know what we think about the good news that Jesus brings: that we who follow will be up to our necks in it, in the life of the world Jesus came to set free, taking big gulps of the cup. But I do know what I see around me. Plenty of greatness among us. People driving friends to the doctors, bringing meals, picking up mail. Band members, tooting their own horns, not to call attention to themselves, but to serve the glory of the football team, marching in weather that causes fingers to freeze to their saxophones. Nurse's aides, volunteer firemen, and Little League coaches. Our confirmands involved in YouthServe, the Museum, and Caring House . . .

"Catch people doing good, Pastor," the preaching group advised. "Our community doesn't think much of itself, and we get trapped in the negative. Catch people doing good things. Surprise them." These mentors encompass many in our congregation and community, making the old story of our lives together something both "first seen" and newly connected to the refrains of baptism and communion, full of sacramental meaningfulness.

And volunteers like Ray, our new president of the Golden Ks who has already figured out that there is no real glory or privilege in being president. . . . When I last saw him presiding over his crew at the Senior Citizens' Center, he was trying another tack. He was already up to his neck in it, so he took a big gulp and put

> *himself on the line. "OK," Ray said, "I'm going to be there at 6:30*
> *Friday night to sell tickets. Who's going to join me? . . ."*

I paste Ray back into the story, but through Ray I sing a song of Jesus with themes of faith. Ideas like servant leader, glory of the Cross, or simply Jesus' self-giving love as a ransom for many become real and concrete ways of being in this world. They become a song we can sing together.

> *Today Jesus punctures the balloon of our inflated ideas of what*
> *service will be like. He acknowledges that we can't know 'til*
> *we've experienced it ourselves, and he promises us that if we*
> *follow him, we will be up to our necks in the fast-flowing stream*
> *of life, drinking the cup of intense joys and sorrows, involved in*
> *the life of the world. But Jesus doesn't send out the troops. Jesus*
> *takes a leaf from Ray's book as servant leader and says, "I'm*
> *going to Jerusalem, to the Cross and beyond to open the door to*
> *a new way of life" and, looks back over his shoulder to see who*
> *else wants to come, who else wants to follow where he has led*
> *the way . . .*

Jesus' and Ray's open-ended invitation aims out the doors of the church into the world where this sermon will have to live. Texts demand closure, but the song of the bard leaves us with the question of whether we will follow. What will happen next, back in the action of the marketplace? We enter the story here, and we write its next chapter, the next chorus of this epic of God's love.

THE ROAD

Larry's and my sermon has a story too. This sermon's coming to birth bears the marks of what it portrays—the rough work of opening a road in a wilderness. Its course was not smooth, easy, or painless, but it was lively, worthwhile work.

Back in the castle, back in the commentaries, its shape seemed clear. Third Isaiah contains rich passages about devastating ruin and the hope of restoring the Temple and a return from exile. These could be juxtaposed with the Temple leader's sense of a distant rumbling, a bulldozer being fired up in the John the Baptist story. Eventually, that bulldozer would bring down the Temple they had rebuilt and buttressed with their culture and power structure. It would bring it down low for reformation in the new creation Jesus would come to embody.

When Larry's friends crowded around this viewfinder, our cruise took us through high ground and swamp—the times our own lives had been like the ruined cities that God had restored. Kevin recalled his brother's death in a car accident on his way home from Kevin and Mary's wedding reception and the road through this desolation that strengthened his faith. Our high schoolers, Courtney and Kip, were reminded of the homecoming of Pastor Cy, the beloved director of the Bible camp. They had eagerly anticipated his return from California, and they were shocked to discover that illness had left his body a ruined city. At his death, they proclaimed the funeral celebration a vision of God's restoration and Cy's new life.

The bulldozer that was poised next door to demolish St. Mary's Church had caught everyone's attention. Paul and Carol shared their experience of being "exiled" from St. Mary's sister church when it had been closed and finding a new home here with us.

I was summarizing my ideas: juxtaposing the situations of the exiled and the established community around the themes of ruin, restoration, change, and God's shaking. I was tying them to some rumblings in our congregation about moving to every-Sunday Eucharist and making other changes in our worship. But just about then, Kevin broke in, frustrated. "You're making it sound way too deep," he said, "way too hard! Marketplace [preaching] should be easy. It should be something everyday that people can relate to, the kind of sermon you could daydream through for a minute or two, but you could still get back into it when you woke up!"

"OK," I said. "As simply as you can, in words you think you could use to tell your neighbors, tell *us* the good news you've found in our discussion tonight." Kevin eagerly began: "My life has been like a destroyed city. You just have to have faith. If something bad happens, look forward to the year of the Lord's favor. Work to lift up others. The wreckage should build your faith stronger."

When it was Kip's turn, he said, "We all have hard times, cities that crumble. But persevere. Eventually, God will save us. God is always there for us."

For Norma, the good news was that "if there is loss, God will bring rebuilding and restoration; if there is change, it is God's shaking."

Paul suggested that, "Whatever you do, life is a matter of renewal. You need to examine it, or you get stale."

Courtney reflected and said that "although Cy's death was devastating, his funeral was a party, and his family is doing great because of their trust in God and the future."

This *was* simpler than the way I saw it, simpler than the way I thought the texts portrayed our situation. At first, I thought that perhaps I needed simply to connect these statements of faith to something larger, but in time (though not in time for this sermon), I came to see that Kevin was looking for "emotional expression," not "emotional introspection."[12] It was a matter of fitting forms. Hard-living in this hard-living place, these people are looking for something that will help them through the night and get them up in the morning. Kevin and Larry are looking not for an intellectual *tour de force* but as Tex Sample puts it, a "faith language of trust and assurance."[13] Already Kevin is linking his language of faith—the faith that is from his heart, comfortable on his lips, and what he will remember—with the words from the Scriptures that struck a chord and fit into the song he wants to sing, the sermon he will preach back in the marketplace. Kevin is naming grace. And I heard an echo of this sermon as it would be heard back in the world in which it has to live.

Now I waited. I waited for the demolition for Saint Mary's Church so that I could connect what was happening around us to these texts and these words of faith. I lunched at the Senior Citizens' Center, and Saint Mary's members told me stories about their church, their loss. We watched as rafters arrived for the new town hall, a sign of hope that new life is being raised up in our community. And the bull-dozers just sat there as they had for weeks. I could tell the Cy story, but it was too fresh, too hard. It was Wednesday. I went back to the texts. Who knows how these things happen, but suddenly driving bull-dozers and preparing roads jumped the gap. I phoned Bruce. You already know that story. Now, I had to work out what to make of it.

I had intended to start with the biblical story: I would draw in local images of exiles on this road, returning home only to find smoking ruins. I'd mention the religious leaders who appeared on a foggy river-side to inquire about the vague earth tremors they were experienc-ing as droves of Jewish faithful beat a path to be baptized by John. They arrived only to hear about a new road that was being cut. Per-haps it was drawn from their own marketplace imagery of roads built for the procession of a statue of a new god.[14] I might work in trial aspects of the John the Baptist story, including the question raised for the Johannine community, the community of returned exiles. It is a question we face every day: God, or an idol?[15] I would link it with the testimony of the group members.

But that Friday I was seduced by the immediacy of the experience of opening this road with Larry; I was caught up in the concreteness of truths already there in what I saw, what I heard—God revealed as the center of all life. Like Matthew, the trained scribe who uses the new as the key to appropriate the old for the present community, I shamelessly lifted images from the texts that I connected with the road-building experience. I decided not to concern myself much with communicating their original context. I painted from the whole can-vas of the John the Baptist tradition, drawing on harvest images that appear in Matthew and Luke but not in John—images that had sug-gested themselves to me in the logging setting. The road making recalled earlier imagery of the Isaiah passage that concerns valleys exalted and hills made low. I aimed for the chopping block, fitting the form of the sermon to the experience of the text through its genre.

Announcements of salvation traditionally come in the "poetic prophetic" voice, proclaiming and blazing a road down which we see Jesus coming. Isaiah used poetic vision to point, as John the Baptist pointed, to "God's word as a dynamic, destiny-shaping presence in the midst of history. We grasp . . . Isaiah's prophecy aright when we recognize its dynamic witness to the creative, redemptive activity of God that occurs within the real stuff of human experience and world history . . . it utilizes the language most appropriate for such a vision . . . the language of poetry, replete with metaphors and mythical allusions."[16]

The language of poetry is the language of images. Like the language of orality, it is also recallable and usable in the places where most people's announcements of salvation will have to be made. Whereas a story evokes images that make it memorable, "images invoke the narrative that gave it birth."[17] They help us recall what we heard so that we can retell the story. Images are multidimensional, like the multiverse of scripture, allowing room for our differing experiences and interpretations within commonspace. Like metaphors, images become vehicles for the "seen and unseen" worlds to collide, split open, and reveal God as the center of all this life.[18] Images are multisensory, engaging our emotions, and our reactions to the sights, sounds, smells, tastes, and feel of things. Images draw us into the story, actively engaging us in completing it, filling it in, and anticipating the next scenes.[19] Stories that we are in, that we are enacting, practicing, and completing in our imaginations, we may more easily remember.

I resolved to go for that small question, the "simple" sermon during which Kevin could daydream: What is the effect of being called by John to be the people who get the road ready for the Lord? Given our community's experience doing this kind of road building in the wilderness, how can we—as loggers, as pioneers who cut homesteads out of the woods, or just as weekenders who need roads into their property to build hunting camps—see this call going out for us in a new way? While it is not always uppermost in our minds, the underlying question of how we meet God in the midst of chaos, despair, and disruption is on our minds every day. It is an Advent question, the advent that is not just a season but also an experience of Jesus' real presence. Could this sermon participate in the shaking, the roar, the freshness, the disruption, and the newness of life that our bodies—our whole selves—experience in the road building to which we are called in John the Baptist's announcement? Could this sermon create a vernacular that would name its grace for us as Larry, Kevin, and our other friends had already seen it?

How does a sermon happen? How do we "set the gap" for the spark of the Holy Spirit to make the lively connections that will reveal Jesus' real presence? "It is as hard for a preacher to say how this is done," writes Barbara Brown Taylor, "as it is for a painter to say how a tree takes shape on a canvas. Do the leaves come first or the branches? What combination of yellow and blue makes such a bright green? How do you make it look so real?"[20]

Is the work of the sermon, after all our careful crafting, a mystery even to us, scribes trained for the kingdom of heaven? Perhaps it is akin to the competence Larry shows in his daily work behind the gears of his bulldozer, alert to what's ahead but blind to the immediate future, teasing out rocks more by feel than by sight. Perhaps it is akin to the knack and vision Annie Dillard finally developed—a kind of courage to lift the ax and swing right through the wood with truer aim. Perhaps preaching is just such an act of faith, just such a work of God. "Lift up the stone, and you will find me there," says Jesus in the Gospel of Thomas, "Split the wood, and I am there."[21]

Come, Lord Jesus. Come, Holy Spirit. Come, pickup trucks.

NOTES

1. Ong, *Orality and Literacy*, 41–42. See Crismon, "Preaching the Truth," 87–93, for a discussion of Ong and orality in preaching.

2. Herbert, *The Parson Preaching*, in Lischer, *Theories of Preaching*, 52.

3. Wilson-Kastner, *Proclamation 5*, 26.

4. *Ibid.*

5. Stoffregen, "Note 612."

6. *Ibid.* Stoffregen reflects on Donald Juel's thought.

7. Wilson-Kastner, 26.

8. Ong, 34.

9. *Ibid.*, 36.

10. *Ibid.*, 42.

11. *Ibid.*, 43–45.

12. Sample, *Ministry in an Oral Culture*, 23. "This confidence in God, *no matter what*, gets expressed by oral people in proverbs and stories, and in very concrete operational language . . . 'God won't give you more that you can bear' . . . 'God bats last' . . . 'you just gotta trust God'. . . ."

13. *Ibid.*, 83.

14. Brown, *The Gospel According to John I-XII*, 43.

15. Ricoeur, "The Hermeneutics of Testimony," 131–34 and 136–142.

16. Hanson, *Interpretation Commentary: Isaiah 40–66*, 190–91.

17. Eslinger, *Narrative and Imagination*, 144.

18. Keir, *The Word in Worship*, 83.

19. Wilson-Kastner, *Imagery for Preaching*, 78, and Miles, *Image As Insight*, 45.

20. Taylor, *The Preaching Life*, 83.

21. Miller, *The Complete Gospels*, 328

Up to Our Necks: Ray Westphal, President and Servant

James and John ask to sit on Jesus' right and left in glory. (Mark 10:35–45)

Just the night before, Ray Westphal had been installed as president of the Golden Ks. I wasn't there, but I know that it was preceded by dinner at Alice's. I know that there was a great turnout to offer support for this service Ray pledged. And I imagine it was one of those glorious mountaintop experiences when it seems possible to accomplish anything.

The next morning, though, I was at the Senior Citizens' Center when Ray was wishing that he had a gavel to bang down to bring the Golden Ks to order. Behind him, a set of wooden letters spelled out P-R-E-S-I-D-E-N-T. Just a few hours earlier, he had received that gift amidst applause and encouragement. Now, Ray was in it up to his neck.

One thing for sure, he figured out how to quiet down the crowd without a gavel. All he had to do was ask for volunteers. Some Golden Ks were needed to sell tickets at the old-time dance at the museum on Friday night.

Silence swept the room. When the talking resumed, people acted as if nothing had been said, and they began to make other announcements about service projects in the community. "OK," Ray tried. "But how about ticket sellers for Friday night?"

When the talk resumed, it was with offers to do something else instead. Maybe a few would come Friday morning and help take down tables.

I can't be sure exactly what Ray was thinking at this point, but I did wonder whether he had known what it was going to be like when he stood up there at Alice's and said "I will. I am able" to serve as president of the Golden Ks.

The Jesus of our story today would have been able to sympathize with Ray. Not too much earlier in the gospel, he, too, had stood on a mountaintop—with Peter, and with James and John. God's voice had showered approval over Jesus, naming him God's beloved son. Moses and Elijah had stood to Jesus' right and left in the power and the glory.

But they go down from the mountain, and Jesus gets down to business with the disciples. "We are going to Jerusalem, and there I will be led like a lamb to the slaughter, mocked, scourged, spat upon, and killed. And after three days I'll rise."

Jesus doesn't actually ask for volunteers for this project, but I imagine his announcement was met with the same deafening silence. And James and John start talking about something else. They come forward, ahead of the other disciples, and they ask Jesus for the places Moses and Elijah had had on the mountain—the right and left sides of a Jesus in glory.

Jesus shakes his head. Obviously, you don't know what you're talking about. You don't know what *I'm* talking about. Are you able to drink this cup? It's strong stuff! Heady stuff! But it will lay you out. Are you able to be with me when the waters overwhelm us, when we're up to our necks in it, and there's no way out but through it?

James and John are like *gung ho* recruits who are done with basic training and eager to get into the glory of battle. They are not thinking about dying or being wounded but about the myth, the romance, the uniform, and the medals. They can't possibly know what they are getting into and what it will be like when the shells explode. What it will be like when they drink of the cup of the intensity, the strong stuff of life, when they find themselves in it, up to their necks. When they are face-to-face with blood, terror, sadness, and the pain that is in the world. When they find out that serving is harder than they had thought. And that the joys are different from what they had expected, are found in dependence on one another. It's a different kind of strength. And glory is not there for all. Maybe for some. But if it is there for you, chances are you will have suffered on the way to it. There's no substitute for experience, thinks Jesus, looking into the future. If you continue to follow me, you *will* get into the strong stuff. You *will* be in up to your necks. You *won't* be able to escape it.

But, says Jesus, the right hand and left hand . . . once you get in there, if you're still thinking about glory that way, if you haven't lost the civilian mindset of wanting to be served, if your training hasn't broken you of that and made you a servant—to country, humankind, your fellow soldiers—if you're still an individual who can't lean on someone else, and look out for the others around you, you will fail at the mission, or you have already failed.

By now, though, there's dissension in the ranks. The rest of the disciples have caught up, and they figure James and John for glory hounds, wanting to be next to the big guys in shining glory, dangerous to them all in their self-serving attitude. Or, maybe they wish *they* had been first to think of asking for special assignment.

Jesus gathers his troops. You know, he says, how you hate it when others look down on you to pump themselves up. Or when blowhard politicians do something generous only when it makes them look good. You know how you hate the way those who look out for number one always seem to end up on top at the expense of someone else. Why would you want to re-create this when I can do something new with you?

Among us, Jesus explains, the values will be different. For us, it will be as among equals. We'll drink our cup together at a round table—no head tables here. The lowly will be lifted up, the mighty will stoop down.

Glory may be bravery on the front lines. Or it may be the army nurse who works seventeen-hour days or a woman stateside who loses a finger working in a munitions factory. It may be the soldier who gives up his life by falling on a grenade to protect a buddy. It may just as well be you, offering yourself for service and never being called. The service of a prisoner of war or of the volunteer who packs a Red Cross box for a POW are of the same value here, Jesus says.

You will all be up to your necks in it. You will all be drinking from the same heady, strong cup of the stuff of life. Among us, every gift we bring, every time we offer ourselves to liberate, every time we serve to set another free, each will carry the same reward. For, Jesus said, "the Son of Man came not to be served, but to serve, and to give his life a ransom, for many."

I don't know what the disciples think about Jesus' words but the next thing that happens is that a blind person receives his sight. I don't know what we think about this good news that Jesus brings, that we who follow will be up to our necks in it, in the life of the world Jesus came to set free, taking big gulps of the cup. But I know what I see around me—plenty of greatness among us:

- People driving friends to their doctors, bringing over meals, and picking up mail;

- Band members, tooting their horns, not to call attention to themselves, but to serve the glory of the football team; marching even in weather that causes their lips to freeze on their flutes or their fingers to freeze to their saxophones;

- Nurse's aides who with kindness and dignity do backbreaking and unpleasant work for those who can no longer do for themselves;

- Volunteer firemen and Little League coaches; our confirmands, involved in YouthServe out at the Bible camp;

- Volunteers at Saint Vincent de Paul, the Prison Camp, Mission Bible, the Museum, and Caring House;

- And volunteers like Ray, the new president of our Golden Ks, who has already figured out that there is no real glory or privilege in being the president but, God willing, there is some honor.

When I saw Ray last, presiding over his crew at the Senior Citizens' Center, he was trying another tack. He was already up to his neck in it, so he took a big gulp, and put himself on the line: "OK," Ray said, "I'm going to be there at 6:30 Friday night to sell tickets. Who is going to join me?"

If anyone joins him out there, they'll discover what Vanessa did in her first volunteer experience. We found her in the kitchen this week at a benefit supper, up to her neck in dirty dishes, the sweat beading up around her hair. "After talking about these lessons last week," she said, "I was really excited to find somewhere to volunteer. You know," she said, her face shining with joy (or perspiration), "this work is a lot harder than I thought it would be!"

Today, Jesus punctures the balloon of our inflated ideas of what service will be like. He turns our notions of glory inside out and levels the playing field by lifting up the humblest act as being as valid as a mighty one. He acknowledges that we just can't know something 'til we've experienced it ourselves, and he promises us that if we follow him, we will soon enough find ourselves like Ray, Vanessa, and all the others who serve: up to our necks in the fast-flowing stream of life, drinking the cup of intense joys and sorrows, involved in the life of the world.

But Jesus doesn't just send out the troops. Jesus takes a leaf from Ray's book as servant leader and says, "I'm going to Jerusalem, to the Cross and beyond, to open the door to a new way of life," and he looks back over his shoulder to see who else wants to come, who else wants to follow where he has led the way.

Those who follow will be transformed like James and John. They finally saw in Jerusalem the glory of the Cross and the power of new life in the resurrection. Transformed, when they find themselves involved in the life of the world and its suffering and pain, they *will* be able. They'll know why they are there and what will get them through. It is love. Love for the world God loved, the world for which Jesus died and rose. Amen.

Chapter 5

The Sermon as Preached:
Keeping Us Awake

THE FIRST LESSON

The Spirit of the Lord God is upon me, because the Lord has anointed me to bring good tidings to the afflicted . . . to comfort all who mourn; . . . that they may be called oaks of righteousness, the planting of the Lord, that he may be glorified. They shall build up the ancient ruins, they shall raise up the former devastations; they shall repair the ruined cities, the devastation of many generations. . . . I will greatly rejoice in the Lord, my soul shall exult in my God; for he has clothed me with the garments of salvation, he has covered me with the robe of righteousness. . . . For as the earth brings forth its shoots, and as a garden causes what is sown in it to spring up, so the Lord God will cause righteousness and praise to spring forth before all the nations.

—Isaiah 61:1–11

THE GOSPEL

And this is the testimony of John, when the Jews sent priests and Levites from Jerusalem to ask him, "Who are you?" He confessed, he did not deny, but confessed, "I am not the Christ." They said to him then, "Who are you? Let us have an answer for those who sent us. What do you say about yourself?" He said, "I am the voice of one crying in the wilderness, 'Make straight the way of the Lord,' as the prophet Isaiah said." . . .This took place in Bethany, beyond the Jordan, where John was baptizing.

—from John 1, *RSV*

So, the sermon hymn comes to a close with a somewhat steady amen, and the organist gestures the choir to sit down. . . . In the front pews, the old ladies turn up their hearing aids, and a young lady slips her six-year-old a Lifesaver and a Magic Marker. . . . The preacher pulls the little cord that turns on the lectern light and deals out his note cards like a riverboat gambler. The stakes have never been higher. Two minutes from now, he may have lost his listeners

completely to their own thoughts, but at this minute he has them
in the palm of his hand. The silence in the shabby church is deafening because everybody is listening to it. Everybody is listening,
including even himself. Everybody knows the kind of things he has
told them before and not told them, but who knows what this time,
out of the silence, he will tell them?

—Frederick Buechner, *Telling the Truth*

The sky is not all that light when we gather for Sunday morning services this close to the winter solstice. A few early arrivals are twist-
ing around, chatting with friends in other pews, trying to catch up
with one another, their voices blending into a sleepy murmur. The
organist is just about to crank up the prelude ("Wake, Awake," is what
I hope it will be), and the door opens, ushering in a blast of December air. Stamping their snowy feet, an exuberant mob breaks into the
tranquillity of the somnolent church.

Larry is leading the pack. "Hiya, Pastor. We made it!" he exclaims.
Just behind him are the rest of the crew, only a little worse for the
wear of the birthday celebration, only a little apologetic for their
dishevelment. "We came straight from camp," they announce, grinning. "Larry's been bragging all weekend that the pastor came out
bulldozing with him, so we got up and decided to come." Larry says,
"I had to bring you this. I took the film right in." And there I am in
the picture. Smaller than I thought I'd be. And sure enough, there
is the road.

This is how the sermon that Larry and I framed so carefully came
out. It is not perfect. It is a parish pastor's, a parish community's sermon from the marketplace. It is a little messy, like life, a little
disheveled. But suddenly, the sleepy room is alive, awakening.

Paul is teaching us a new hymn with his guitar: "My Lord, What a
Morning." We are singing the end of the chorus—*when the stars
begin to fall*—as I step up to the pulpit. Larry and his whole family,
including his one-year-old granddaughter, Toni Lu, are spread out in
three pews to my left, grinning expectantly. Toni Lu's parents are
pulling out crayons and bags of Froot Loops, but we all know that
these won't contain her for long.

Bruce takes one more sip of coffee and sets the cup, provisionally, on the windowsill. I take one more deep breath. I take in Larry, the crew from camp, Lily and the widows, the confirmation kids in the balcony, Toni Lu's parents with their hands full already. "Grace to you, and peace," I begin. "From God and from our coming Savior in Jesus the Christ. Amen."

❦

SERMON

Preparing a Road

"Anybody you know of making logging roads?" I asked Bruce. Who else?

"Well," he said, "you could call Larry. I heard him on the radio today calling for a bulldozer up Smokey Lake way, so I suspect something is happening up there. But don't forget, it's sauna night."

Right, I thought, and started calling as soon as it seemed reasonable that Larry would have come out of the steam bath and had his fill of Grandma Lu's biscuit. I caught Larry just as he was coming in the door. "What are you up to tomorrow? Will it have anything to do with a bulldozer?"

"Yup," Larry answered.

"Not cutting a new road in the wilderness by any chance, are you?" I asked.

"Well, not a new road," Larry said, "but I'm opening one up."

"So, can I come and watch?" I could hardly wait.

It is Advent, our season of expectation and anticipation, a time of preparation and praying down a savior into the midst of a chaotic world. To help us get ready,

I needed to go out and see for myself what Larry was up to in the wilderness—like the Temple leaders who came by to check out John the Baptist. They didn't find out about John on the CB, but they might have suspected something was happening, something was up, just by the rumbling of the crowds beating a path into the wilderness of Bethany to be baptized by John. "So what are you up to, John?" the priests, the Levites, and the Pharisees asked. John answered them in the words of the prophet Isaiah: "I am only someone shouting in the desert, 'Get the road ready for the Lord!'"

It's Ken Steiro, actually, who makes that call at the Ned Lake offices before sunrise. "The time has come," he announces, pausing over his cup of hot coffee, "The time is ripe for the harvest of maples and cherries and yellow birch. Get the road ready for the loggers. Make landings and skidways and places to park the pickup trucks. Prepare the road!" And because Larry is going out into the wilderness to get the road ready, Larry is the one who takes me to find out what it might be like to prepare for God's harvesttime. I went with him to discover what we are up to this Advent as we prepare a way for Jesus to come to us on the road; and to discover what God is up to with us in all the seasons of our lives.

Out with Larry, I found out what a lot of you already know. Making roads, even with a bulldozer, is hard work and it starts early. I found out that it pays to dress warm and tough. As we go to work, making roads for our Savior to come, as God makes roads for *us* in this season of Advent, our garment of salvation may very well be well-oiled flannel and our robe of righteousness a Carhartt jacket.

Making roads is costly; it's an investment, a risk. For us; for God. Forty thousand dollars had been shelled out even before this road could be opened, in anticipation of the harvest to come. God offered us love while we were yet sinners. But how do we prepare this road into the wilderness? Where do we start?

As we set out, Larry tells me about a quieter day, cruising the land on foot. Jerry Jarvi had been there to mark the boundaries and blaze the trees that were ripe, valuable, ready. "Now," says Larry, "you look for the road. You look for it by imagining the straightest way through the smallest trees. Look for the openings." He points. "See," Larry says, "the road is already there, really, waiting to be discovered." You prepare for the road by beginning to imagine the road, looking for its shape, expecting it.

Larry shows me his map—what the land looks like on paper. "Rings," he says, "are hills. Little furry circles," he says, "are swamps." "If you say so," I say. "It gives you an idea," he says. "But I like to come out here and walk it myself." Preparing the road, he charts the path over high ground and around swamps and makes choices that take into consideration the blazes that mark out what is of value and the boundaries that mark costly trespasses.

Larry pulls out the other tools of his trade, tools that keep him on track: his compass, to set the course, and the sun chart, which tests his orientations for any magnetism from the iron ore. It's magnetism that might give him false readings and mask his true position on the earth. This is Larry's work during the Advent season. He spends some time quietly discerning, making choices, finding out where we stand, getting our bearings from the sun, and noting boundaries, blazes, and the value of things. He is preparing the road in the wilderness for the harvesttime that is coming.

But it is not all quiet time. When Larry fires up his Caterpillar and gets to work on the road, the whole earth begins to shake and tremble. The Cat's mighty roar fills the air before he gives me a pair of little yellow earplugs. But even they are no relief: they only drive the roar and the rumble right inside of me. It's exciting—and scary.

Larry lifts his blade high and begins. There is no road opened in the wilderness without disruption and change. The spruce tree shudders in surprise and shakes off all its snow before it crashes to the earth. The poplar topples, splinters, and cracks, offering up its roots and secret places. Lofty treetops brought low become just so much brush. Making a road, or even getting one ready, changes everything. It changes the whole landscape.

Disruptive as it is to prepare the road, it is also . . . fresh. The evergreen scent of crushed balsam reminds you of Christmas and all its anticipation of what is coming down the road, a hope for the future even in the midst of the wreckage. Eventually, the brush pile of treetops becomes a new playground and shelter for squirrels and chipmunks and other forest creatures.

Larry stays alert to widowmakers, to what's ahead, even though he can't see all that much right in front of him over the hood of the dozer. He's working by feel if not by sight. I am just getting used to the bone-shaking roar when it all—suddenly—stops.

Larry interrupts our road building with an announcement I've been waiting to hear. "Guess what!" he trumpets into the sudden silence. The whole earth seems to be awaiting his news. I take out my earplugs. "I almost forgot to tell you. The baby's coming! Jim told me over the radio this morning. He and Betty are already on their way downstate. Karen is in labor." No longer just an idea, a hope, a prayer anymore, Karen and Tom's baby was making its way into the visible world, and Jim and Betty were on the road to meet it!

"Coffee break time. Let's celebrate!" Larry brings out the coffee and doughnuts. "Every day a picnic in the wilderness," Larry says. If everything I was experiencing hadn't seemed like such a new world, it might have seemed odd that Larry was setting up a small feast in the middle of nowhere, in tribute to a baby's birth. Is this, a table spread under the lightly falling snow, what God is up to in Advent? A picnic in the wilderness in all times and in all places, even amid the wreckage, even in the middle of labor?

Back to work. The rumble resumes. Larry moves the blade down low and digs into the earth. He plows, making a new way. It is ugly and painful, this scraping the earth raw, making this scar in the landscape. It is noisy, hard work, cutting into the forest. I can't stop thinking about Karen, laboring toward new life, a way being made through her that will change her forever.

Widening the way, Larry slices through a hundred-year-old white-pine stump. Our ancestors have walked this way before us, with horses and sleighs and crosscut saws. Atop the ancient stump, a new shoot has grown, a scraggly but proud little balsam. The power of new life pushes into the world; the generations rise and fall.

Disturbing as it is, this road making is also beautiful. Alongside me, the earth rises up dark brown. It looks like modeling clay formed and reformed, turned over, over turned, as a way is made. Bright ferns and tumbled moss make surprising splashes of green, displaced, and tossed up into the snow on our new edges.

Something is making me excited: the news of Karen's baby making its way into the world . . . and the smell of spring. When Larry prepares a road in the wilderness for the harvesttime, it smells just like my garden smells when I dig it up after its winter slumber. The smell of the overturned earth is the smell of new life, the promise of renewal in the face of disruption. Come summer, new shoots will spring up, and plants will take root. But meanwhile, the new opening will harden with the cold and become serviceable. A road will be ready for those who depend on this wilderness for labor and harvest and food on the table. Perhaps even a deer or two, weary of the haunch-high snow this winter, will use this path and nibble on the tender branches now brought to their level along the roadway. Every day a picnic in the wilderness!

Is it possible that as much as we want to defend against Advent's message that something new is happening to us, that change is on the horizon, that a babe is making its way into the world and that this babe is opening up a road through and to us, that we will not be able to resist the excitement? Is this the way God comes to us? In this change that is God's shaking? In setting a table even in the wilderness? In this realization that in times of loss, God can bring rebuilding and restoration? That we can trust in God's future, looking forward to the year of the Lord's favor and living in it even in the midst of chaos?

Out in the woods with Larry, I learned what many of you already know about getting a road ready: When we hear the voice shouting that it's time to prepare the road for the Lord, we need to be prepared to make an investment and see the time ripe for a harvest. In the church and the world, with our time and our dollars, we will work to harvest cherries and birches and maples, and all the different kinds of people who are ready to be gathered into the circle of God's love. This is what we're up to this Advent.

We'll dress warm and tough in the garments of salvation, our baptismal robes of righteousness. We'll go out cruising through our high ground and our swamps. We'll use the eyes of our faith to discover the best openings—the road that is already there for us in the wilderness and the One who looks to meet us on that road. We'll choose a path that leads to the justice God loves, guided by the blazes and boundaries, our compass and our sun chart, our tools of the trade in our Bible and in the faithful witnesses of all time. We'll make landings and skidways and spots for the pickup trucks to park, making openings for other people, practicing hospitality, lifting others up, supporting them in their work. Every day a picnic in the wilderness!

And something around us will be opened up. Maybe even us. We may find ourselves uprooted and disrupted even as we experience the freshness of the new thing being done for those who are depending on the harvest. We'll know the promise and power of new shoots springing forth. We'll know what it is to be molded and remolded. We'll be hardened to withstand the traffic this new road is made to bear—the travelers who need rest, the small creatures who find food and shelter on the road's margins, the God who is coming to meet us there.

This is the only way the road is made. With skill and work. With disruption and openings. With a roar of power and the exhilaration of freshness and newness of life. With faith in God's promises and future even when we can't quite see over the hood.

The announcement breaks into our world today: The time has come! In the wilderness, make straight the way of the Lord! The babe we've been waiting for is already here! Amen.

❧❧

In what was to be the moment of silence between the closing hymn and the postlude, Matthew, Bruce's boy, is first down the balcony stairs, the thundering herd of confirmands right behind him. "Looks like I'm dressed for Advent!" he tells me, shrugging the shoulders of his Carhartt jacket and pulling meaningfully at the knees of his Carhartt pants. I am impressed that he forgoes the usual tapping of his watch and the announcement of how many minutes the sermon imposed upon him.

Kevin comes through the line after them with a shy smile. "Well," I ask, "were you able to do any daydreaming today?" "Oh yeah," he says. "I could just see John the Baptist, just like Ken, pointing. 'Go make a road here, go make a road there. Do this next. Go see that guy." I am certain I'd never used the word "pointing" in my characterization of either one. Yet Kevin has perfectly appropriated the nature of John the Baptist as portrayed in John's Gospel. He is pointing to Jesus: "Go see that guy."

Another member of the congregation simply shakes my hand, addressing me as "lumberjack." Larry's family marvels that the announcement of Karen's and Tom's baby had intersected with the road building and the Advent readiness for the birth of a savior, and they say how "personal" it had made the Advent message. They are all on their way back to camp, and they roll their eyes, telling me how they will have to endure, for the rest of the weekend, Larry's bragging about being in the sermon.

Later, when the preaching group got together, we speculated that since the church next door was still standing, it must have been God who had led us out into the woods to find true common ground with our logging congregation. Norma really liked the compass: "It reminded me of the Bible, and following our Savior for direction in our lives and its wilderness." Carol thought it was a great message that, through turmoil and disturbance, new roads can be opened:

> *We felt the quiet peacefulness of the forest and then the sound of the ground being torn up by the bulldozer. We felt the vibrations. One of the high points was the total silence for the announcement of the baby's birth—the coming of new life. The silence of the woods and the food served in the wilderness were strong images. We were reminded that our personal life can be in shambles but we can find an inner core of peace through faith. The ending of the sermon was great!*

Low points in the sermon, they thought, were too few people in the landscape and too many words in some of the images. Remembering Toni Lu's presence and her parents' struggle to listen, we recognized that the sermon has to be "easy" enough not just so adults can daydream, but also that they can stay with it when small children begin to run and scream.

I still had to drive to my second service. Back in the sacristy, I found another sermon comment form:

> *I enjoy all sermons, that touches at home alot, or guide me through the times. What we deal with, the ups and downs of our lives, work, home, friends, family. Didn't know much of logging, but could understand to what happens in our life. What I do, to get ready. And with God. What the ups and downs are that our*

*faith is one of the same, that will carry us through, some day,
our faith through Jesus Christ, peace will be with us. God is
always with us, working with us. We don't always realize it.*

I read it again. What was it that Jim Nieman had said? "If the message we sing is ever to leave the confines of the church, it must be borne through the lives and voices of those who hear it, who may sing it quite differently than we would, but in ways perhaps more appropriate to the world than we might ever imagine."

I pick up the form and set it next to the picture Larry gave me. The road looks great. "Make no mistake about the ability of our hearers to detect whether we know their songs," continues Nieman. "In a thousand subtle ways we telegraph to them our respect of their experiences or lack thereof."[1]

After his family had filed past me, Larry had given me a big hug. "You remembered everything I taught you," he said, beaming. It looked like he might say more, but he just gave me another squeeze and followed the gang out the door and down the road.

NOTE

1. Nieman, *Preaching That Drives People From Church*, 112

Chapter 6

A Mirror for the Northwoods and a Window on the World: Living the Sermon

Preaching is an act of the Church in which the substance of her faith is ever freshly declared and reinterpreted in the lives of men who live within the instant and changing actuality of history.
—Joseph Sittler, *The Anguish of Preaching*

We were asked to draw pictures of our role in the community, as opposed to verbal articulation. I drew a picture of a mirror since we reflect (or try to) our listening audience, as well as being made up of many volunteers within the same community. Standing alone, however, it reminded me too much of "navel contemplation" so I leavened it with "window on the world" taking into account our national and international program content.
—Walt Gander, WXPR (NPR) Station Operations Director, on the development of his station slogan

Now when they saw the boldness of Peter and John and realized that they were uneducated and ordinary men, they were amazed and recognized them as companions of Jesus.
—Acts 4:13

Helen, our organist, is one of the last to leave church the Sunday of the bulldozing-with-Larry sermon. She opens the door into the snow flurries, but before leaving, she turns back to tell me, "I just can't wait until tomorrow morning rolls around. All those guys will be firing up their big machines, and they won't be able to stop thinking religious thoughts!" Tickled, she takes this picture with her out the door.

Helen's forecast makes me smile, too, as I turn out the lights, turn down the heat, scoop the sermon off the pulpit, and dump it on the pile atop the file cabinet. It would take me about ten more seconds to open the drawer and slip it in the folder marked "Advent 3." But I don't. I treat it almost as if it's a loaf of bread I expect to rise just a little more.

Here is another story about Martin Luther: At preaching day's end at the castle church in Wittenberg, he would walk home to enjoy a glass of ale "while the Word did its work."[1] I wonder whether when he toasted that Word at work, he ever lifted his glass to the likes of Larry, holy to the Lord as he fires up his bulldozer. Or to Matthew, as he slips into his Carhartt jacket, dressing for school and for Advent. Or to Kevin, as he pours his morning coffee while his boss gives him the day's instructions and finds himself somehow unable to shake the picture of John the Baptist pointing down the road, to Jesus.

The contents of this chapter lie just at this horizon into which the road surely winds but begins to disappear from my view. This is the chapter that Larry and his friends write after I've gone home for my ale. It's about the preaching that is to be done in the marketplace. There, the sermon, the Word at work, will take forms and shapes that I might barely recognize by the time the church secretary, wondering why I couldn't have taken the ten extra seconds to open the drawer, ends up filing those pages for me. This story is not that sermon but the one that gets out of the church as we look for Jesus to meet us in the commonspace of life. Down the road a ways, we catch a glimpse of some of the gifts of preaching from the marketplace:

- Discovering a "something more" that reveals God's presence in the midst of our lives

- Tending the fertile ground of the community's experience from which a theology might grow for witness in this place

- Affirming the vocation of the baptized

⚘ Remembering the vocation of the parish preacher

⚘ Recognizing the Word as a mirror and a window for our lives

⚘⚘

DISCOVERING A "SOMETHING MORE"

Helen was surprised to hear that she was going to be in this story. I had to remind her of the comment she had made that Sunday as she was going out the door. "You know," I said, "about how all those guys were going to fire up their big machines and wouldn't be able to stop thinking religious thoughts."

"Oh," she replied, tilting her head skeptically. "Did I say that? Well, maybe they did—for a *day* or so."

I realized that it had been a while. In fact, a couple of years. Still, had these gleanings been mine alone? I did wonder sometimes how long Matthew might have associated his Carhartt jacket with a garment of salvation and how useful that association might have been in the larger scheme of his life. What had happened to these sermons, these lives, around that bend into the future?

Drinking his glass of ale, down the street from the castle church, a self-satisfied Luther says something, I suppose, about his confidence in the Word at its work. But wasn't he ever curious? Did he never slip back down the road to the marketplace to see whether he could catch a glimpse or an echo of this working Word?

I caught Larry after church as he was going for coffee. I wanted to find out what, if anything, had stuck with him from our day in the woods. I just came right out and asked him whether the sermon that we'd worked on together had made any difference in his life?

"Aw," he said, looking down at his feet, "now you're asking me to talk!"

"Well, you don't have to come up with something right this minute, and if it honestly hasn't had any effect, that's OK, too. Just think about it for me, will you?"

Uncomfortably, Larry took a step back and scratched his neck. Asking him to talk, to reflect, went way beyond the original bargain to take me bulldozing. Nevertheless, Larry is the kind of man who would give up the shirt on his back. So we stood outside the church and together we tried to squint down that road we'd prepared.

"There is one thing," Larry started. "It's just small. I don't know if this is anything. But what sticks with me is the smell of the dirt. I smell the dirt now."

I nodded. I, too, could smell again the freshly overturned earth from that day. Larry checked out my reaction and went on. "And the trees. I smell the trees, too. But mostly what I think about is the smell of the dirt. It wasn't until that day, when you were sitting up there with me that I ever thought about anything at all. Then when I heard you talk about it that way in the sermon. . . . Before it was just . . . *natural*, you know? But now, it means more."

The world Larry lives in is material, concrete. He builds roads, he makes great homemade noodles and sauce. But, of course, what I wanted to know was what the dirt means for him now. Larry shook his head, working to put into words that which doesn't come to him as words.

"Well, the other thing I've thought about since the sermon that day is how perfectly it worked out. I mean, that day we went out, my job was to open up a road that had really overgrown. This summer I've been working on really wide-open roads, and that is more like snow-plowing. It wouldn't have been like what you talked about. And then Karen's baby coming. Sometimes I think about that. How it worked out that way, so you could preach that sermon, when it might not have.

"I don't know what it means, though. It just means . . . *more*. I notice things now. Like how the dirt smells. I enjoy it more now. Sometimes

I'm sitting up there on the bulldozer, and I notice. I enjoy it." He took a deep breath. "It means more."

Larry was right the first time. The meaning for him *was* the something more. The meaning was a something deeper, an inspiration, the discovery that a thing in his natural world *could have* meaning.

Perhaps the gift of marketplace preaching is that it helps us notice. It inherently invites awareness of a depth and fullness of meaning where God might be found in the real, material world. Larry, his work, the dirt—what he and I thought of as the concrete or finite realm—might actually be capable of bearing meaning, taking us into those deeper places, revealing the world of the infinite, holy to the Lord. As we prepare this road, we are also opening ourselves to the full dimensions of our human lives. On this road, Jesus comes to meet us as the Word, revealing meaning, a something more: God's presence in the commonspaces in which we live; God as the center of all life.

Larry is not that explicit in words, at least not to me. But he is noticing. He is wondering. He is sitting up there in his Cat breathing, enjoying it more. He may even be squinting a little, cruising, charting his road through high ground and swamp that suddenly *have meaning*.

"Rocks," Larry concluded, as we walked to our cars. He let himself enjoy my quizzical expression before he answered it. "I notice the rocks, too. When I hit the rocks and have to work them out without being able to see them? Now I always think of you."

TENDING THE FERTILE GROUND FROM WHICH THEOLOGY GROWS

"Ah, the smell of the new road!" Paul, a preaching-group member, emailed me not long after we'd worked together on this sermon. I had asked him how things had been going since he'd left the counseling center and gone into business on his own. Now he had a new way to express his experience of a new venture. And I had a new way of understanding that this meant dimensions of birth, death, resurrection, and epiphanies of God's presence all at once. In connecting our everyday language with the language of faith, we had created new commonspace in which to meet and talk, in trust and hope, about the events of our lives.[2]

Now we can smell the dirt, and it has become something more for us, a way of going deeper. How does that dirt—and the experience of faith that begins to be linked with it through preaching—become the fertile ground from which a theology may grow for a community?[3] Bruce and Trapper Charlie showed me the way.

Old Trapper Charlie was a good man in the woods. He lived a loner's life in a one-room cabin on the Net River; trapping, fishing, and hunting for his simple living. The world in which Charlie lived had passed on before he did: the fur market had collapsed; the Fur Rendezvous, where tales and pelts had been swapped, had closed; the good men in the woods had gone back to the earth like fallen timbers. Trapper Charlie, all but blind and crippled with arthritis from long winters and icy rivers, was cherished for the sake of the past he represented. Those who remembered looked in on him from time to time and listened to the old stories.

A fire call awakened the community one night in early spring. Trapper Charlie's shack was going up in flames. Volunteer firemen had raced their pickup trucks as fast as they dared down rutted roads, but they stood helpless before the blaze. In vain, they searched around the cabin, looking for tracks, for signs that somehow Charlie had escaped. Those who were able, as soon as they were able, went in for Old Charlie. They found his body halfway between the woodstove (which they had all, at one time or another, seen him start up by throwing gasoline on the coals) and the door. They speculated that this time, being blind, he had just missed; and being lame, he just hadn't made it.

The community asked Bruce to be the one to say a few words at Trapper Charlie's funeral. They had asked my husband, Fred, to do a simple burial liturgy, but they wanted Bruce—a logger, a volunteer fireman, a good talker, the son of a trapper—to speak. Though I had no official role, Bruce had asked me several times whether I'd be there. I slipped into the back pew just as the evening service started.

I saw before me a sea of plaid, in wool and flannel. Our congregation has never been what you'd call formal in attire, and Trapper Charlie had not been "churchy." He'd never been a joiner, and the gathered mourners reflected these traits. In deference to the prayers Fred was now leading, hats had been removed from heads I had never before seen bared. But Fred was on his own for the responses.

The crowd settled more comfortably when Bruce stood up for what began as a eulogy. He recalled the heritage of Trapper Charlie and of his own father, John, who had trapped with him. He raised for us the whole host of good men in the woods. Our little church was the market square where this epic was being performed in Charlie's honor. In our peculiar Finnish with a French Canadian twang, Bruce sang us songs of the forests, rivers, and legendary hunts, with refrains in which everyone could join.

Then he told us the story of that awful last night. He told it as you tell an old tale to those who were there—to those who already have heard the tale many times over coffee, over beer, at the café, and at the bar. He told it to those who had already told it themselves. We all knew how this story turned out. But this time, Jesus was in the story, too.

The story of the firemen's search became for us the story of Jesus, who comes to find Charlie and saves him. At the place in the telling where everyone knows and expects Charlie's friend to come heartsick upon the body, Bruce told instead of Charlie's joyful reception by his friend Jesus. Scooped up and led out of the blaze by this friend, Charlie is no longer blind or lame. Bruce ended this story with Old Trapper Charlie and Jesus snowshoeing down the frozen Net River together. Jesus is pointing out signs of beaver and showing Charlie the way. They are sharing a plug of chewing tobacco over some old story when they disappear from our view.

The funeral lunch was held not in the church basement but around the corner at the Hotel Bar. Some of the conversation was about

Charlie and days gone by, but a lot of the talk over beers was of the good news Bruce had told them: about the comfort and peace, the wholeness felt in the service. One woman painted the picture of her own late husband into the healing story Bruce had told. She was sure now, in a way she had never been before, that her husband had been on that walk down the Net with Jesus and Charlie. She was able to see her husband with Jesus for the first time. These are the fragments of salvation, the echoes of the Gospel, wherever the dead are raised and good news is preached to those who have gone wanting for it.

Sitting in the pews, I'd begun to get a glimmer of why Bruce had been so eager that I be there to hear him preach. There was a certain familiarity about the way Bruce's Jesus showed up in the story of our community. It sounded an awful lot like the Jesus who had come from some place like Covington, turned up at the Hotel Bar for Fish Fry, been detected in the daily work of people like Rob and Lois, surprised us at the casino, and been anticipated on our own logging roads. Bruce was holding up a mirror, reflecting a marketplace sermon as preached on Sunday mornings.

But his sermon had also sounded its own declarative note of such a sermon as *lived*. It had opened a window into a depth of understanding for the substance of faith and life as it is lived and expressed in this community. When sermons are conceived in the soil in which they will have to take root, we shouldn't be surprised that our church becomes the market square into which everyone is welcomed, the Hotel Bar can become the venue where people talk about the good news, and everyday people like Bruce are recognized as companions, people who have broken bread with Jesus.

AFFIRMING THE VOCATION OF THE BAPTIZED

Bruce's sermon for Trapper Charlie was a gift of good news offered for a gathered community. But most of those who gather for Sunday's Word don't do this kind of preaching. Most who are driven from church by the preacher's aim through the pews and out the doors will be living out their baptismal vocation to be more literally "the Word at work."

"I have been thinking of your last e-mail," Lois writes. I had visited her at work at the Genesee Street Clubhouse for the sermon from Habakkuk, the sermon in which she became a billboard for the good news and our work of sticking out our arms for those who run by us in despair. Now she gives serious consideration to my invitation that the congregation write this chapter about how the sermon continues to live for them:

> *Working with you and the others from the group made me more aware of where I fit with my job, the people I work with, and my family.*

> *Your visit at the clubhouse helped me see things I knew were there but was too overwhelmed with the politics of the job to notice anymore. You opened my eyes to the job I really do, and I continue to carry this with me. I do believe we sometimes have to fill in for Jesus. It still gets hard, especially now when my part-time coworkers are struggling with hour cuts and ongoing conflicts between management and employees. I find I can still be calm and offer support and remind them of the goodness of Jesus. Life isn't always full of roses, and when it is there are still thorns in the roses. But you don't even notice them when Jesus is walking with you because he makes you more aware and thankful.*

> *. . . I do realize that having Jesus in my life doesn't make the problems go away; it just makes them seem so much less overwhelming, and I can find the calm to look for solutions instead of only focusing on the problem.*

> *I have to get ready for work so will let you go. Have a wonderful day. Lois*

Lois, like Larry, is noticing the events of her daily life and work in a way that has opened her eyes to the something more—the depth of human and faith experience that she is able to name as Jesus' presence. Lois's work in the world is in a "helping" profession, where it's relatively easy to make explicit connections with Jesus' work of healing and raising to new life. But Mike, Lois's husband, wonders how he connects. As a mechanic, he stands under cars all winter, gritty slush dripping on him while he makes sure our brakes work well. But he comes home from my Habakkuk sermon asking if what he does at work makes a difference in anyone's life. What does he do that would earn him recognition as someone who breaks bread with Jesus? Lois reminded me of Mike's need to see himself and his work mirrored in these sermons, too. She suggested that in preparation for the cemetery sermon, along with the funeral directors, I should also talk to Bill.

Bill is a second- or third-generation vault builder and gravedigger. He started in the business at the age of sixteen, when one of his uncles retired. Bill's last name, he tells people, means "grave" in Finnish. He makes it a practice not to do the work on the graves of family members. Bill pours vaults in his backyard right up until hunting season, when the cemeteries close to winter burial. When the spring thaw comes, he knows that some days there will be a dozen burials, leaving him little time for pouring vaults or anything else.

There are five setups, Bill explains, "to make a grave look good." He works hard at it. "My business is very touchy. Things have to be perfect. A strap can't break, for instance. It's a very upsetting time for the families. Things just have to go smoothly."

As Bill tells me about his work, I picture him and his crew members as I have seen them at the grave side. Ever since he noticed Fred and me digging under his green carpets looking for dirt to cast on a coffin, he has always made sure to set aside a little cup of sandy earth for us. He brings it from the truck in what must have been the gold-toned cap of a spray paint can, made holy to the Lord for this purpose. From that point on in the service, I picture Bill and his crew standing at a discrete distance. Hats off. Hands respectfully laid one on top of the other in prayer. They are all but invisible while the "professionals" go about their work of comforting the family in the ritual. The crew remains on the sidelines until the last family member, thanking the funeral director and me for "a lovely service," leaves for the funeral lunch. If I look into my rearview mirror as I drive away, I see Bill and his crew moving their equipment back in to do the burying.

I think about Bill and the strap he makes sure won't break, and I realize that in his competence at work, Bill also saves lives.[4] I have never thanked Bill and his crew for having made sure that the service was lovely, that a strap has not broken, that I have not fallen into the grave as I spread my dirt in the committal. By virtue of their careful work, they have been an invisible but critical part of the caregiving team.

Such competence, a not-so-simple dedication to one's job, is also the Word at work, the vocation of the baptized. This is the word I hope Mike will hear more and more deeply as he stands beneath those slush-dripping cars this winter: God has inscribed holy to the Lord on Mike's forehead in baptism, and his daily work is more surely consecrated as Work of God than that of the bells on Zechariah's horses. Our work in the real world matters. It means more. It saves lives.

Preaching from the marketplace has helped us find ways to see ourselves preaching good news by performing our work—whatever it is—competently. Attending to our work is a "good work," a bold witness of the ordinary that earns us recognition as people who have broken bread with Jesus.[5] Such a ministry of presence, the sometimes invisible but real presence of a Word at work in our world of grave diggers, bulldozer operators, and mechanics, also bears witness to our faith with stunning eloquence.

In the Acts story about Peter and John, everyone is amazed that the man who is able to heal and proclaim is not a trained scribe but an ordinary person who has broken bread with Jesus. Even more interesting, though, is that in each of the stories about Peter and John, it is only Peter who seems to be saying or doing anything worthy of recording as witness. Yet, Peter and John who are always *recognized together* for their boldness of speech. Together they are credited with healings in Jesus' name. Perhaps John is just "the Church." Perhaps he is there as a reminder that none of us ever acts or preaches alone.

Preaching that is conceived in the marketplace takes seriously this partnership of preaching as an act of the Church. It has to be Larry and Kim, or Mike and Lois, just like Peter and John. There are no senders and receivers to make up subjects and objects in the marketplace preaching economy, only ordinary people who have broken bread with Jesus. Marketplace preaching gathers ordinary people around texts and sends trained scribes into the community on field trips to root the sermon in the places where the sermon has to live, cutting across dualisms and hierarchies. Preaching from the marketplace has at its foundation a respect for the multistoried aspects of scripture's witness and the multiplicity of gifts and perspectives brought to the roundtable. This partnership, as well as the sermons created within these "gaps" of otherness, becomes lively space in which God might move through our lives and the world.[6]

Preaching conceived in the marketplace goes on to be the Word at work, reinterpreted in a material world where the substance of the church's faith is tested and has to live. Wherever this fresh declaration takes place—at kitchen tables, the Hotel Bar, and Bible study; under the car lift at the garage and in the supermarket; at the busiest intersection in town and in the pulpit—preaching is an act of the Church.

REMEMBERING THE VOCATION OF THE PARISH PREACHER

Carol Jean, a new member, dropped me a note after the marketplace sermon on "Every time we think of you we thank our God" (Philippians 1:3). We had been taken around the community to see the gifts of good news each of us brings through our work in the world. Carol wants to bless my work, too, with an "And also with you."

> *Just a little card sort of saying: Every time we think of you, "we thank our God." You not only preach the word of God, but you live it outside the church. You really show us the important role we do stand for not only in our homes, but also out in the community. It has really opened our eyes and heart to the Lord! Sincerely, Carol*

Sometimes even the trained scribes or householders can get themselves recognized as companions of Jesus. Carol's note opens my eyes, too, to how my perception of my work has changed. Ministry is less fragmented. I am no longer torn by choices about visitation, Bible study, or sermon preparation. Preaching from the marketplace makes it all of a whole. My job. *My* work of God. Now it all means more. I enjoy it more.

Preaching from the marketplace is like getting out of school to go on field trips. Ministry gains freshness, excitement, and fascination for the workings of the world that such outings always have offered. Preaching from the marketplace gives me time, energy, and a mandate to make the visits I have always wanted to make. In a world where people are increasingly uninterested in a home visit from their pastors (with all the cleaning up, coffee cake baking, scheduling gridlock, and small talk that has burdened it), marketplace visits offer different opportunities. People are excited to find their pastor simply available in their midst as they trace the busy paths of their days.[7] They are grateful that their pastor comes to learn about their work, if only to find out why church council meetings need to be over by 8:30 on work nights.

Preaching from the marketplace also makes me accountable for visits that I never got around to making. Or, more honestly, I should admit that I was intimidated by the thought of making. I had to ask Vanessa to sponsor and introduce me into the group of teenagers hanging out in the parking lot. I asked Bonnie and then Nancy to take me to the casino. "I'm getting all teary just thinking about it," Bonnie said. "I am just so grateful and amazed that you are even willing to do something like this. It might be so helpful to us spiritually."

Visitation that accompanies marketplace preaching is purposeful in this way. It is situated in places where people are confronting real-life issues and have something to talk about. In these common-spaces, the pastor's ministry of presence brings awareness of the possibilities for interface between God and world, between faith and work; we take part in pastoral conversations that otherwise never seem to materialize. Nancy and I talked about God and gods on our way home from the casino. I heard about how a logger might view timber as trees actualizing their potential, allowed to be useful for the world. I heard veterans talk about glory, service, love, sacrifice, shame, and God, in ways that challenged my long-held perceptions about military service. In these commonspaces, I discover what it's like to hear my voice sounding puny outside the church. How difficult it might be sometimes to witness to our faith in God's grace, in the world of works.[8]

When pastoral visitation for marketplace preaching takes place over coffee at the kitchen table, it gives rise to conversations about matters of faith and life. Who brought you closer to Jesus? What was stewardship like in the 1930s? Visitation becomes the something more that opens a window to the depth and fullness of human experience, and it reveals that God is already present in those deeps, the center of all life.

Trust, also, is sounded in those depths. I discovered not only God in the deep, but also my own people's love for me. I discovered their eagerness to invite me into their lives, into this colorful world, breaking me into that story that I had longed to enter. I discovered how deeply I was trusted, trusted to honor their stories, to tell them well. Almost unfailingly, I told people they might or might not end up in that week's sermon. Almost unfailingly, they gave me blanket permission to use my best judgment, and they trusted me not to embarrass or misrepresent them.

Like Larry, I notice things more. The love and the trust. The dirt. Mike and Bill. Jesus, snowshoeing around the bend for us. The black and white of text has become living color; I see moving pictures instead of stills pasted into a crumbling old album. I notice that "Can anything good come out of Nazareth?" sounds like a Covington joke.

Noticing that, I realize there is probably a lot more going on in the scriptures than I had thought. I look for this, and recognize a whole host of associations the first hearers of these stories would have made between the spare lines of text. I can't always know what they are. I don't know exactly what it means that "it was winter, and Jesus was walking in the Portico of Solomon." But I have an inkling that it is something more than an incidental detail. I notice what it *could* mean just because of the tone of Lu's voice as she tells me about sacred time and space when the geese touch down on Cemetery Lake come spring and fall. I notice more and more such places in scripture.

I get an inkling of what Jesus and the gospel writers were doing in the unspoken, undeveloped, yet lively spaces of the text. Putting myself into the scene when Lily tells me that Arvo and his dump truck brought her closer to Jesus, I am able to fill in the blanks with that host of associations that are our commonspace. I see that the gospel writers gave us that lively space so that we could put ourselves into the story. I'm starting to see that my work as a trained scribe is to learn precisely where connections need to be made across the gap and where gaps need to be left for sparks to fly—to make room for us in the story.

For instance, when Toivo and Eino finally end their search for the Messiah at the Hotel Bar's Fish Fry, I get a glimmer of the whole sermons that are implicit in the Bible stories that tell us exactly where Jesus is eating and drinking. We may not fully understand the social implications of the places Jesus appears in first-century Israel, but we can get the subtlety of where he sits at the Hotel. Anyone who has ever stood at the door trying to decide whether to sit at the bar on the left, the booths on the right, or in the dining room around the corner, will appreciate the whole sermon preached into our tacit understandings of social location and privacy simply by noting that Jesus is sitting at the booths, within earshot and sight of those at the bar, and he does not retreat to the dining room.[9] Having learned this, I expect these lively spaces in the gospel story to mean more as I go cruising, looking for the boundaries, squinting for the road, and marking my blazes along the path through the high ground and swamp.

Kip, one of our high-school students, looks over my shoulder and offers this forecast for my preaching life: "I think you will continue in this way of relating sermons to the everyday marketplace of our community, and over time you'll become expert at relating everyday events, common and uncommon, to the workings of God in our lives today." What a wonderful prophecy not only for the parish preacher, but for all God's people.

RECOGNIZING THE WORD AS A MIRROR AND A WINDOW

We end where we began, crowded around the viewfinder of the text, the lens of our life in this place. We are still squinting for the road, aiming to see Jesus there. When I gather the group members to see whether they can help me look beyond that horizon down the road we have prepared, I discover that while I have been going to their work sites, they have been visiting my workplace, too.

This is what pretty nearly all the group members tell me about their experience: one of the best parts was gaining insight into the sermon-creating process. Most had never really thought about where a sermon might originate. "It was exciting," says Lisa, "being in on preparing the sermon and then seeing how it actually ended up." "I think I will understand sermons better from now on," adds Kevin, reflecting on his experience of seeing sermons woven out of our work together.

Courtney, a high-school student, has become more interested and more confident. "I found that I *can* understand sermons. I often zoned out and couldn't catch the meaning. . . . Placing my friends and me in a more familiar setting helps our age-group pay attention!" Norma, on the other end of the age spectrum, also gained in self-assurance through the experience. She says, "As the oldest member of the group, at first I was worried that I wouldn't have anything to offer. I had never even discussed a sermon in depth. I did a lot of praying, God listened, and it got easier because the sermons were great."

Gary now listens for the diversity he experienced as the group gathered around the texts. He says, "Every church member should realize the effort it takes to deliver a message to a congregation made up of the many cross sections of society. After all, the purpose is to have an impact on every individual life."

Stacy thinks the process wouldn't work without the marketplace piece, which "transcribed stories from the lessons and gospels into situations that are real and plausible to me." The sermons helped the gospel become a recognizable reflection of her own life. But the gathering around the text also made the sermon "more" for Stacy: "When you're there reviewing and understanding the lessons better, the sermon has more meaning. I imagine most people just hearing the lessons for the first time as they are read can't appreciate the small things such as a history of location or history of certain people. And a pastor can't cover that in depth in a short sermon." Kip agrees. "It really gave me the experience of learning how to digest the Old Testament readings and figure out what they mean and how to relate them to my life." Gary, too. "I'm developing an inquiring attitude toward the gospels and how they relate to me."

"This experience has awakened my faith," says Norma. And now she wants to share it: "Hearing marketplace language in the middle of a Bible story and bringing ordinary events into conjunction with scriptural teachings, showed me how the good news of Jesus can be spread in everyday situations in everyday language. By hearing Scripture in everyday language, we find it on our own lips. It is easier to practice evangelism on a one-on-one basis if we have the necessary words."

Lois found that gathering around the lessons and becoming apprenticed to others propelled her into both recognizing the witness of others and feeling free to share the good news herself:

> *Our common experiences brought us together, and sharing together, we were able to see that we are all God's children and we are all family. . . . Studying the Word with others and hearing how common our feelings are makes me so much more aware of the words in the Bible and how it does fit into our everyday lives. . . . I am even learning from the consumers I work with: So many of them are so full of good news, and they don't hesitate to share it with me. You would not believe how often the Bible and the wonders of it all come up in our conversations at the clubhouse. I used to try to steer away from this for fear that I would be overheard by the wrong management person, but now I don't do that: Everyone needs to hear the good news, and it is OK to relate how even our everyday lives are so full of blessings. We just have to learn to recognize them.*

Lois is getting bold, and I bet if the wrong management people do overhear her, they will recognize her as a companion of Jesus.

Cruising through the texts together, or, as Lisa would put it, "finding that others shared our same fears and hopes," has helped us see ourselves in the story we long to break into. Preaching from the marketplace has proved both a mirror for the stories of our lives and a window into a world of "something more." In this mirror, we can see ourselves in familiar settings, as God's people, living in everyday ways. We can see the reflection of the good, the bad, the ugly, and the beautiful as they exist in the places and people with whom we live. When we framed this mirror with the gospel story, we have been able to see the something deeper of our human lives lived in a world made holy to the Lord. This framing turns the piece of glass from a mirror into which we might be tempted to "navel gaze" into something more like a window through which we may step into the world of the gospel story and see ourselves living in that world as well, the world beyond ourselves, the world that God so loved.

❧❦

"So what of the sermons have you remembered? What has made a difference in your lives?" I began asking, after talking with Larry. Norma went first. Right away, she said "Get a road ready for the Lord" was, for her, the most vivid sermon. "John the Baptist did it in the Bible, and we did it too. Our work on the sermon helped our congregation get ready for the changes of every-Sunday communion." "Do the Toivo and Eino sermon again," begged Kaye. Norma liked that one too. "Their search for the Messiah was both humorous and meaningful." "The cemetery sermon," Deb said. "Listening to all those names. And there were strong images."

A sermon written from a DNA lab touched Fran, who works as a hospital lab technician. "I never thought that I'd be able to talk about my work with my friends at church. I thought I was doomed. I'd have conversations at church that had no real understanding of the ethical dilemmas I face at work, as well as conversations at work that had no real understanding of the ethical dilemmas I face because of my faith. I look for more opportunities like this now."

Lynn and I talked about the casino sermon. It troubles her that there are people at her work who think grace is cheap. She thinks that people need to be told clearly that there is right and wrong, that God hates some things. And she tells me about others who were upset about this sermon. They had hoped, for the sake of their loved ones who spend too much time in the casino, that I would condemn it. "If Jesus had actually come to that casino," they said, "he would have turned over the tables of those money-changers, too!" I was surprised. Most of the people who had commented on this sermon at the time—both gamblers and those against gambling—had told me that it had given them something to think about. I was about to get defensive, and I told Lynn that as a result of the way I had approached the topic a woman had gained the courage to ask me to talk and pray with her about a possible gambling addiction. But I realized that I had preached this sermon three years earlier, and it was still memorable enough to give us something real to talk about over lunch. I can't feel bad about a sermon like that. The Word is most certainly still at work.

NOTES

1. Lueking, *Preaching*, 118.

2. Margaret M. Mitchell, who teaches New Testament at the University of Chicago, helped me understand that while marketplace preaching relies on local vernacular, it can also be instrumental in creating a vernacular—a vocabulary about faith, a vocabulary available for locally common use.

3. Schreiter, *Constructing Local Theologies*, 40.

4. Diehl, *The Monday Connection*, 31. Diehl describes a ministry of competency . . . "that we do our best at what we do, and it saves lives."

5. Tappert, *The Book of Concord*, 78–9. In the Lutheran tradition, excellence at work as the vocation of the baptized is described in Article 27 of the Augsburg Confession: "For this is Christian perfection: Honestly to fear God and at the same time to have great faith and to trust for Christ's sake we have a gracious God; to ask of God, and

assuredly to expect from him, help in all thing that are to be borne in connection with our callings; meanwhile to be diligent in the performance of good works for others and to attend to our callings."

6. Rose, *Sharing the Word*, chapters 1–3, but esp. 78, 136, n. 6, and Chopp, *The Power to Speak*, 59. I believe that this process of gathering people around the Word, taking it out into the spaces in which God is moving through our human lives and landscapes, and preparing the sermon with an eye and an ear to ways in which it may be preached in the commonspaces of our lives may be the bridge between Chopp's and Rose's vision of mutuality and solidarity in the "gap."

7. Simmel and Sitze, *Hints for Making Workplace Visits*.

8. Diehl, 80.

9. Miles, *Image As Insight*, 34, 8, 36. Placement or context in visual images "speaks."

Toivo and Eino Meet the Messiah

Eli helps Samuel hear God's voice (1 Samuel 3:1–10)

Philip invites Nathaniel to "come and see" Jesus (John 1:43–51)

Toivo and Eino came in the Tall Pines. They greeted Nancy and Eileen, who were going out just as they were coming in: "Ya it's a little crisp today, you betcha hey." "Howdy, Carol Anne, Howdy, Candy," they called out as they walked into the Pine Cone Café. Toivo and Eino sat down to the stools, and without even askin' Gretchen started pourin' the coffee and Karen warmed up their blueberry muffins. Before you know it, the place started to fill up. Stanley came by, and the Jarvis and it was a snow day and in came Jack and Ester and the grandkids. "If you stay long enough, just about everybody comes through here," says Gretchen, comin' round with the coffee.

Toivo and Eino ask, "Hey, what's up?" And there's talk of a lost load over by Channing there and how cold it got last night and Sarah's weather picture on the TV and the kids' report cards coming out and the sledding over to Muncie's hill and who saw Pastor Fred at the post office this week and the annual meeting over at Bethany on Sunday and the Packers.

Then Eino tells Toivo, "Hey, guess what? We found the Messiah this week."

Toivo says, "Ya, sure."

"No, really," says Eino. "I went over to the Senior Citizen's for lunch and Edith and Joe and Lily were there."

"Edith and Joe were back?" asks Toivo.

"Ya, couldn't take the warm weather down in North Carolina."

"Ya, you betcha."

"Anyways, I sat down with Reino and Waino, you know, those guys who always hunt 'n' fish somewhere north of Amasa."

"Ya, I know those guys," says Toivo.

"And we're talking about the blizzard coming and the school bond issue and the annual meeting over at Bethany on Sunday, and the Packers."

"Ya, the Packers," says Toivo.

"Ya, well, so, pretty soon they get to talking about that John—you know him, he's up north there, too, and goin' around in deer hide and livin' off the land?"

"Ya, he's an odd one," says Toivo.

"Well one day this guy comes by, and John says, 'He's the one. He's the one to follow. The Savior.' So, Reino gets his brother Waino and they follow him thinkin' they'll at least find maybe a good fishing lake but what they find is— the Savior."

"Ya don't say!" says Toivo.

"'Ya sure!' I says too, but they say to me, 'Check it out,' and sure enough, right there over Sandy's scalloped potatoes comes the guy Reino and Waino are talkin' about. And he's the guy, I'm telling you. And hey, you'll never believe who he is!"

"Who is he then?" asks Toivo.

"It's Jesus, Joe's son, who works over there in the sawmill. Helmi's second cousin's nephew, from up Covington way."

"Ya sure," says Toivo. "Can anything good come out of Covington? You know, Eino, they just got that gas station but we have the gas station *and* a laundromat in Amasa."

"Well, maybe it's Watton, actually," says Eino. "But, hey, check it out. I'm tellin' you, this is the guy! Check it out for yourself!"

So Eino takes Toivo to Fish Fry at the Hotel Bar, and sure enough, there's the Becks and Brenda and Jessica and Ian and Craig. And they're talking about the confirmation retreat and raisin' teens and the annual meeting at Bethany and, the Packers. And sittin' there in the booth is also Jesus, who always enjoys a good fish fry.

"Check it out," says Eino.

"Hey, Toivo, my friend," calls Jesus, "You're an honest guy who tells it like it is, and you're a good fisherman, too."

"Ya sure," says Toivo.

"No," says Jesus, "Really. I've asked around about you. I saw you in the bleachers at the Forest Park game with Jordan and Leanna. And even before that, Fred Hiltonen pointed out your ice shack on Fire Lake that time when you were praying to God for that big walleye."

"Holy Wah!" says Toivo, "This is the guy. This is the guy!"

"What did I tell you?" asks Eino.

"Oh, Toivo," asks Jesus, "do you believe only because I got you that big lunker? Even Gretchen and Karen know what to get you for breakfast. Stick with me, and you'll see even greater things than that. I want to get to know you more and more, become better and better buds. I want to walk where you walk, know what it's like for you. Talk to me, man. And the more you know me, the better you'll come to know the Big Guy, too. Check it out."

۶⃝۶

"Ya sure," we might be saying. But this must be how people came to know Jesus in the Gospel of John. People are bumping into each other, the people they already know in the places where they generally hang out. Family. People from their own small town. Just telling the news, what's up. And it's no hard sell, either. Whether it's the way John put it—*come and see*—or the way Toivo and Eino put it—*check it out*—it's a pretty easy no-pressure invitation.

In our small town, word travels pretty much the same way it did in Jesus' day. It spreads person to person, by word of mouth, when we run into people having coffee at the café or at the post office or at the store or at a game, or when we talk to people on the phone. We're pretty connected. Mae Wicklund doesn't get out much, but you can't tell *her* any news, can you?

This is just the way that the good news about Jesus can spread—the same way we share the news every day. In the middle of pretty ordinary stuff, God's presence can be made real among us as we make connections. A reminder that there's an annual meeting at church today, or the sledding party is around the corner; or someone's getting baptized or someone we all know is in the hospital or near death. Just inviting someone—someone we already know pretty well, to "check it out" with us can be inviting others to come closer to Jesus. Simply inviting someone to Bible study or worship, to coffee or lunch or for a walk— and reaching out in Jesus' name—can lead to inviting others to follow Jesus or listen for God's call.

Sometimes I think we figure that most of the people we meet around here have already been introduced to Jesus. That might be true, but just hanging around church doesn't mean we can't get wake-up calls to know Jesus better, to see and hear him more clearly. And it doesn't mean that these calls can't come from one another.

In our first lesson, Samuel' mother, Hannah, dedicates Samuel to God even before he was born. After she weans him, Samuel comes to Shiloh where he serves God with Eli the priest. He even sleeps right next to the Ark of the Covenant, the sign of God's presence, but he still needs Eli to tip him off to God's voice and how to respond.

I asked some of you this week about the people in your life who have led you to know Jesus better, and none of you had to think too hard about the flesh-and-blood people who have invited you to follow.

Most everyone told me that their parents had brought them to church, but often there was someone else who woke them up from just sleeping in the faith and helped draw them closer to Jesus.

For Courtney, it was learning to say bedtime prayers at sleep overs at Desiree Ketola's house. Desiree's mother, Bonnie, taught her "Now I lay me down to sleep."

Kip's guitar teacher invited him to open his ears and pay more attention in church.

For Norma, Sunday School in Finnish didn't mean much more than words. Nevertheless, she says the whole neighborhood in farming country helped raise the kids in faith.

Paul and Eino both mentioned their wives as people who had helped deepen their faith, who had invited them to come and see.

Lu was awakened by the groups in Word and Witness and the Prayer Group. Gladys gives credit to Nellie Aho and Phil Kolenda and the gospel choruses they sang during their Bible study in Amasa.

Lily says it would have to be Arvo, who drove her to church in the dump truck. And her daughter Dulcie, who slept on her lap during services. One day, Lily noticed that as Dulcie slept, her hair had gotten caught around the little buttons on Lily's dress. Lily was so afraid that Dulcie would feel her hair being pulled and wake up screaming. Then, all the crabby old ladies would shush her. But Dulcie simply woke up, looked around, smiled.

In these people, in these everyday moments, we can be amazed by the ways God comes close to us in Jesus and invites us to get to know him better. To talk with him. To let him walk close beside us so he can see what it's like for us. It's a great thing to live in a town where people might know us so well that they can start heating up our muffins for breakfast before we even get to the café counter, but Jesus promises us a kind of closeness that is even more rewarding. And as we get closer in our following, we will be more and more amazed by God's glory and God's love for us that Jesus shows us.

We come to know Jesus—or to be awakened in our faith—in everyday ways by everyday people who have invited us to come and see, to check it out. Making this kind of invitation is something we can do. This is something we *already* do. Even Toivo and Eino can handle this. Amen.

Now it's time to put this story to bed. It began with a little boy who stomped on the pages of one of his favorite storybooks and his mother who puzzled over ways to help him break into the story he loved. Sometimes I like to think that the little boy was Wyatt and the mother was Judy. Wyatt has grown up some since his book-stomping days, but Judy still likes to read to him at night. One night she tucked Wyatt into bed, leaving the door open a crack as she said good night. All was quiet, but after a while she noticed some strange flashes of light coming from Wyatt's room.

Judy pushed open the door and saw Wyatt playing under the covers with a flashlight. She smiled, thinking he had his book under there, and she told him to put the book away, to turn off the flashlight, and go to sleep.

"No, Mom. Wait," Wyatt said. "I have to show you something. Look!"

Wyatt held the flashlight to his palm. In the darkness, the light shone through his thin hand, illuminating blood vessels, bones, and the flesh between them. With a big grin, he announced, "See, Mom. It's true. God's light shines through me!"

Judy reminded me that the children's sermon that morning had been about Saint Paul. I had mentioned a flashlight and spoke about God's light shining on Paul in a way that changed his life. After that, I'd said, Paul became a saint, someone through whom God's light shined for others.

During the "kids' minute," Wyatt had been shy about saying what talents he had to share. But right after church, he ran outside and started shoveling the inch or two of snow that had accumulated on the sidewalk. I didn't know whether the big grin on his face was from the joy of his work, from God's light shining through him, or from the way he was making people dance as he shoveled snow between their legs!

That night Wyatt sang out the joy of his discovery. "Look, Mom," he proclaimed. "It really is true. God's light can shine through me!" Wyatt has found himself in the lively space of the story he loves.

The road in Larry's picture winds into the future as far as the eye can see, through quietly falling snow. So does this book as you go on to write the next chapters at the edge of that horizon, the place where Jesus will come to meet us.

❧ Bibliography ❧

Allen, Ronald. *Preaching the Topical Sermon*. Louisville: Westminster John Knox Press, 1992.

Boring, M. Eugene. "Matthew Introduction and Commentary." In *The New Interpreter's Bible, Vol. 7*. Nashville: Abingdon Press, 1995.

Bornkamm, Heinrich. *Luther in Mid-Career 1521-1530*. Translated by E. Theodore Bachmann. Philadelphia: Fortress Press, 1983.

Bozarth, Alla. *The Word's Body: An Incarnational Aesthetic of Interpretation*. Lanham, Md: University Press of America, 1997.

Brown, Raymond E. *The Gospel According to John 1–12*, Anchor Bible Series, vol. 29. Garden City, N.Y.: Doubleday & Company, 1969.

Buechner, Frederick. *Telling the Truth: The Gospel As Tragedy, Comedy, and Fairy Tale*. San Francisco: Harper & Row, 1977.

Byatt, A.S. *Possession*. New York: Vintage Books, 1990. Quoted in Nancy Willard, "Dreams of Jinni" review of *The Djinn in the Nightingale's Eye, The New York Times Book Review*, 9 November 1997.

Chopp, Rebecca. *The Power to Speak: Feminism, Language, God*. New York: Crossroads, 1991.

Crisman, Richard N. "Preaching the Truth." *Liturgy: Preaching the Word, Journal of the Liturgical Conference*, vol. 8, (fall 1989).

Diehl, William E. *The Monday Connection: A Spirituality of Competence, Affirmation and Support in the Workplace*. New York: HarperCollins, 1991.

Droel, William and Gregory F. Augustine Pierce. *Confident and Competent*, Notre Dame, Ind.: Ave Maria Press, 1987. Quoted in William Diehl, *The Monday Connection: A Spirituality of Competence, Affirmation and Support in the Workplace*. New York: HarperCollins, 1991.

Dudek, Duane. "90s 'Romeo' Courts Youth for the Bard." Review of *William Shakespeare's 'Romeo and Juliet,'* by Baz Luhrmann. *The Milwaukee Journal-Sentinel*, 1 November 1996.

Ebeling, Gerhard. *Word and Faith*. Philadelphia: Fortress Press, 1963.

Edgerton, W. Dow. *The Passion of Interpretation*. Louisville: Westminster John Knox Press, 1992.

Eslinger, Richard L. *Narrative and Imagination: Preaching the Worlds That Shape Us*. Minneapolis: Fortress Press, 1995.

Gunsten, Paul and Steven Schwier. *Partners in Preaching: Using Small Groups for Sermon Formation*. Produced by SELECT Video Courses & Lectures for Continuing Education, A Leadership Development Resource of the Division for Ministry, Evangelical Lutheran Church in America, 1999. Videocassette and manual.

Hanson, Paul D. *Interpretation Commentary: Isaiah 40-66*. Louisville: Westminster John Knox Press, 1995.

Herbert, George. *The Parson Preaching*, 1652. Originally published in *The Temple and the Country Parson*. Boston: James B. Dow, 1942. Quoted in Richard Lischer, *Theories of Preaching: Selected Readings in the Homiletical Tradition*. Durham, N.C.: The Labyrinth Press, 1987, 52.

Hilkert, Mary Catherine. *Naming Grace: Preaching and the Sacramental Imagination*. New York: Continuum, 1997.

Jensen, Richard A. *Telling the Story: Variety and Imagination in Preaching*. Minneapolis: Augsburg Publishing House, 1980.

Keir, Thomas. *The Word in Worship*. London: Oxford University Press, 1962. Quoted in Lucy Atkinson Rose, *Sharing the Word: Preaching in the Roundtable Church*. (Louisville: Westminster John Knox Press, 1997), 70.

Long, Thomas G. *Preaching and the Literary Forms of the Bible.* Philadelphia: Fortress Press, 1989.

Lueking, F. Dean. *Preaching: The Art of Connecting God and People.* Waco, TX Word, 1995.

McClure, John. *The Roundtable Pulpit: Where Leadership and Preaching Meet.* Nashville: Abingdon Press, 1995.

McCurley, Foster R. *Proclamation Commentaries: Genesis, Exodus, Leviticus, Numbers.* Philadelphia: Fortress Press, 1976.

Miles, Margaret. *Image as Insight: Visual Understanding in Western Christianity and Secular Culture.* Boston: Beacon Press, 1985.

Miller, Calvin. *Marketplace Preaching: How to Return the Sermon to Where It Belongs.* Grand Rapids, Mich.: Baker Books, 1995.

Miller, Robert J., ed. *The Complete Gospels, Annotated Scholar's Version*, Rev. and exp. ed. Santa Rosa, Calif.: Poleridge Press, 1994.

Nemerov, Howard. *Reflexions on Poetry and Poetics.* New Brunswick, N.J.: Rutgers University Press, 1972.

Nieman, James. "Preaching That Drives People Out of Church." In *Currents in Theology and Mission*, vol. 20 (1993).

Ong, Walter J. *Orality and Literacy: The Technologizing of the Word.* London: Routledge Press, 1982.

Ptomey, K.C., Jr. "A Cry in the Night," in *Weavings* 8 (1993):33. Quoted in Mary Catherine Hilkert, *Naming Grace: Preaching and the Sacramental Imagination* New York: Continuum, 1997, 111.

Ricoeur, Paul. "Toward a Hermeneutic of the Idea of Revelation," and "The Hermeneutics of Testimony." In *Essays on Biblical Interpretation*, edited by Lewis Mudge. Philadephia: Fortress Press, 1980.

Ritschl, Dietrich. *A Theology of Proclamation, 126.* Richmond: John Knox Press, 1960. Quoted in Lucy Atkinson Rose, *Sharing the Word: Preaching in the Roundtable Church.* Louisville: Westminster John Knox Press, 1997, 97.

Rose, Lucy Atkinson. *Sharing the Word: Preaching in the Roundtable Church*. Louisville: Westminster John Knox Press, 1997.

Russell, Letty M. ed., *Feminist Interpretation of the Bible*. Philadelphia: Westminster, 1985.

Sample, Tex. *Ministry in an Oral Culture—Living with Will Rogers, Uncle Remus, and Minnie Pearl*. Louisville: Westminster John Knox Press, 1994.

Schlafer, David. "Serving As an 'Eli' or an 'Elizabeth': Listening Preaching Colleagues into Graceful Speech." Paper distributed at *Preaching as Sacred Play Workshop*, 1997.

Schreiter, Robert. *Constructing Local Theologies*. Maryknoll, N.Y.: Orbis Books, 1985.

Simmel, Sally and Robert Sitze. *Hints for Making Workplace Visits*. A resource produced by Ministry in Daily Life, Division for Ministry, Evangelical Lutheran Church in America.

Sittler, Joseph. *The Anguish of Preaching*. Philadelphia: Fortress Press, 1966.

Smith, Christine M. *Preaching As Weeping, Confession, and Resistance*. Louisville: Westminster John Knox Press, 1992.

———. *Weaving the Sermon*. Louisville: Westminster John Knox Press, 1989.

Stoffregen, Brian. "Note 612," *Gospel Notes for Next Sunday*. Ecunet online discussion (13 October 1997).

Sutera OSB, Judith, ed. *The Work of God: Benedictine Prayer*. Collegeville, Minn.: The Liturgical Press, 1997.

Tappert, Theodore G., ed. and trans. *The Book of Concord*. Philadelphia: Fortress Press, 1959.

Taylor, Barbara Brown. *The Preaching Life*. Boston/Cambridge: Cowley Publications, 1993.

Thistlethwaite, Susan Brooks and Mary Potter Engle, eds. *Lift Every Voice: Constructing Christian Theologies from the Underside*. San Francisco: Harper San Francisco, 1990.

Thulin, Richard L. *The "I" of the Sermon: Autobiography in the Pulpit*. Minneapolis: Fortress Press, 1989.

Tisdale, Leonora Tubbs. *Preaching As Local Theology and Folk Art*. Minneapolis: Fortress Press, 1997.

Tracy, David. *Blessed Rage for Order: The New Pluralism in Theology*. New York: The Seabury Press, 1978.

―――. *The Analogical Imagination*. New York: Crossroads, 1981.

Travers, Peter. "Just Two Kids in Love: William Shakespeare's Romeo and Juliet." *Rolling Stone*, 14 November 1996.

Trible, Phyllis. *Texts of Terror*. Philadelphia: Fortress Press, 1984.

Wilson, Paul Scott. *The Practice of Preaching*. Nashville: Abingdon Press, 1995.

Wilson-Kastner, Patricia. *Imagery for Preaching*. Minneapolis: Fortress Press, 1989.

―――. *Proclamation 5: Aids for Interpreting the Lessons of the Church Year, Series B, Pentecost 3*. Minneapolis: Fortress Press, 1994.